THE POWER OF IDEALS
IN AMERICAN HISTORY

THE POWER OF IDEALS IN AMERICAN HISTORY

BY

Ephraim Douglass Adams, Ph.D.

Professor of History
Leland Stanford, Jr., University

KENNIKAT PRESS
Port Washington, N. Y./London

THE POWER OF IDEALS IN AMERICAN HISTORY

First published 1913
Reissued in 1969 by Kennikat Press
Library of Congress Catalog Card No: 75-85979
SBN 8046-0596-3

Manufactured by Taylor Publishing Company   Dallas, Texas

CONTENTS

INTRODUCTION

The lectures hitherto given under the auspices of the *Dodge Foundation for Citizenship* have embodied the thought of distinguished men, famous in some field of public service,—in law, in state administration, or in church organization. These men, speaking from personal experience, have been able to present in didactic form, ethical standards of conduct. The teacher of American history will certainly affirm that he also has standards of conduct and he naturally turns to history itself, seeking in the experience of the past great principles of national progress. If it can be shown that the American people have been largely influenced in their development by moral principles, or by ideals, it is at least a safe presumption that ideals still animate this nation.

I wish then to recall to your remembrance certain leading ideals, powerful in their influence upon our history, in the past one hundred years. Before undertaking this, however, permit me an explanation of the reason for my choice of subject. There is today a very decided tendency to seek purely material reasons for historical development, and especially so, apparently, in American history. The causes of the American Revolution are asserted

to have been almost wholly commercial, to the
exclusion of those ideals of political and religious
freedom which our forefathers loudly voiced, and
which their descendants have accepted as a creed.
Upon this period of our history I do not propose
to touch, but it is interesting to observe that the
modern interpretation differs little from the contemporary accusations of British writers,—as in the
words of Thomas Moore, expressing contempt for
sordid motives hidden under the guise of liberty.

> " Those vaunted demagogues, who nobly rose
> From England's debtors to be England's foes,
> Who could their monarch in their purse forget,
> And break allegiance, but to cancel debt."

This seeking for the material basis of historical
development is not indeed a new pursuit. Buckle
expressed it in terms of geographic environment,
"The mountains made men free." But it was
answered, "Men who would not be slaves, who
would be free, fled to the mountains." It may be
that when England has become a memory, and
Holland a myth, the advocate of geographic
environment will find in the rocks and in the chill-
ing mists of New England the forces that created
the Puritan conscience, and dwarfed his emotions.
In the sunshine and clear atmosphere of my own
state of California, the kindly critic finds excuse
for the unrest of its people,—and for their warm

impulses. The motto of Stanford University, "Die Luft der Freiheit weht," has an intoxicating effect upon the Eastern tourist, and he frequently becomes a living testimony to the influence of geographical environment. Yes, "the wind of freedom is blowing,"—but as one observer remarked, "It is not a hurricane." The ideals of California are not founded in geography, or in climate. They are founded, as elsewhere, in the spirit.

In truth, students of American history today, particularly the economic specialist, and the geographic historian, are too much inclined to claim for the results of their research, the attributes of an all-powerful, all-compelling force. The careful scholar, though his principal interest be industrial progress, makes no such claim. Bogart, in the preface to his "Economic History of the United States," says, "The keynote of all American history, from whatever standpoint it may be written, is found in the efforts of a virile and energetic people to appropriate and develop the wonderful natural resources of a new continent and there to realize their ideals of liberty and government." With such a statement there can be no quarrel; the concluding phrase is indeed the major premise. But other writers either forget that premise, or deny it. Simons, a determined materialist in history, begins the preface of his "Social Forces in American History" with this assertion:

"That political struggles are based upon economic interests is today disputed by few students of society. . . . Back of every political party there has always stood a group or class which expected to profit by the activity and the success of that party."

And his book is an attempt to prove that throughout the whole course of American history, economic interests alone have determined political action. This idea is developed to the exclusion of all other forces. In short, he asserts the "economic man."

It is this latter extreme contention that I wish to deny,—not by analysis and criticism, but by an appeal to the facts of our history, for a fact, a truth of history, may be something wholly impossible of reduction to concrete terms; it may be an emotion, a sentiment, or an ideal, and as such, so long as it is generally accepted, even though it be directly contrary to economic interests, it may be an all-powerful spring of conduct, and the prime cause of political action. The "economic man" is a fiction. Over seventy-five years ago, here at Yale, in a Phi Beta Kappa address, Horace Bushnell denied that such a man, as the sole moving cause of history, had any real existence. "There is," he said, "a whole side of society and human life which does not trade," and which "wields, in fact, a mightier power over the public prosperity itself just because it reaches higher and connects with nobler ends."

This is not to deny, nor does any one deny, the influence of industries and of geography, in national growth. All that I wish to express is that there are other influences of an intellectual,—it may be a spiritual,—character, and, in a time of undue emphasis upon the materialism of American history, to recall to your memory a few of the great ideals that have animated our national conduct and moulded our destiny. I shall attempt neither explanation nor analysis of these ideals, but rather shall seek to show by straightforward historical review and by familiar quotations from leading Americans of the time, the *force* that was in them. Therefore I have called these lectures "The Power of Ideals in American History," and the topics to be treated are Nationality, Anti-Slavery, Manifest Destiny, Religion, and Democracy.

I

NATIONALITY—A FAITH

I

NATIONALITY—A FAITH

A nation is defined as "a people associated together and organized under one civil government, and ordinarily dwelling together in a distinct territory." Nationality implies a sense by such a people of their independence and their unity, with the patriotic determination to preserve these conditions. In the present time, it is difficult to think in terms not national, whether we regard Europe or America. But one hundred years ago this was far from true. England, France, and Spain, alone of the great powers of Europe, possessed the conditions and the spirit of nationality. The evidence of that spirit was abroad, however, and nationality is rightly held to have been the most powerful ideal of the nineteenth century. More than any other force it wrecked Napoleon's dream of an empire of Western Europe, and as one looks at Vincenzo Vela's wonderful marble, "The Last Days of Napoleon," in the Corcoran Art Gallery, one wonders whether the feeble invalid, with the map of Europe spread upon his knees, whose eyes seem visioning what might have been, may not have recognized at last the force, the ideal, that had defeated him.

In America, the ideal of our revolutionary fathers was independence. But it was not *national* independence. Each colony jealously guarded its sense of separate existence, and independence from Great Britain once assured, each state, in spite of the forms of a wider nation, maintained its sovereignty. Difficulties at home and dangers from abroad forced the adoption of the Constitution of 1787. There were a few men in the convention, and a few also in the country at large, who rejoiced in this first step toward American nationality. Timothy Dwight, later to be one of the greatest of Yale's distinguished line of presidents, was inspired to address the constitutional convention of 1787 in a poem beginning with these lines:

" Be then your counsels, as your subject, great,
  A world their sphere, and time's long reign their date.
  Each party-view, each private good, disclaim,
  Each petty maxim, each colonial aim;
  Let all Columbia's weal your views expand,
  A mighty system rule a mighty land."

But such visions, such an ideal, were not felt by the mass of men. Timothy Dwight in all his views and policies has been rightly described as "an earnest of the nineteenth century,"—a forerunner of his times. The constitution, said John Quincy Adams, was "extorted from the grinding necessity of a reluctant nation," and these words, save that there was *no nation,* accurately depict contemporary attitude. In view of the later "worship of the constitution," it is hard to realize that there was a long period when the spirit of independence, the fear of a centralized government, made men suspicious of, and even opposed to, a real American unity. Nearly ten years later, Washington, in his farewell address of 1796, gave three lines to the topic "liberty," taking it for granted that love of *liberty* was securely planted in the hearts of the people, while nearly one fifth of the entire address was devoted to arguments showing the value of a permanent Union of the states. This was indeed his central thought, evidence of his fear of a new separation of the states.

I shall not follow, step by step, the growth of the sense of American nationality. It was a gradual development, hastened at the last by the patriotic fervor evoked in the second war with England,—the War of 1812. Defeated though we were in that war, our capitol burnt, our ports blockaded, our shipping driven from the seas, we emerged triumphant, not because of our success in a few naval duels, or of Jackson's belated victory at New Orleans, but because, cutting loose from all dependence on European alliances, trusting in our right, and exhibiting our willingness to fight for right, we had given notice to the world that we were a *nation.* But the greater triumph was

over ourselves. By 1815 the sense of nationality
was established,—not so firmly as to escape grave
danger in the future,—but still sufficiently established to have become a recognized ideal. To the
astonishment of the oldtime conservatives, and to
the dismay of many a politician accustomed to play
upon the local jealousies of the people, there had
arisen a belief in national destiny, a sense of remote-
ness from older nations and older customs, a consciousness of a separate and distinct existence for
America, in short, an ideal of unity and of nationality. Let us see what force this ideal had, how it
was expressed, what its influence was, in our later
history.

The Monroe Doctrine of 1823, warning European
powers that the United States regarded the American continents as no longer subject to colonization,
and protesting against a concert of action to aid
Spain in recovering her revolted dependencies, was
a notice served upon the world that we had become
a nation. This was the application of a new ideal
to conditions outside our territory. But the real
test of the new force came from within, when it
was brought in conflict with the divergent interests
of different sections. When separate states lose
their individuality in union, when a nation comes
into actual being, one of the most vital evidences
of that union is found in the willingness to adopt
a general, rather than a local, system of taxation.

Thus the question of federal taxation in the United States early assumed an importance greater than the mere matter of revenue. A tariff system on imports promised to give needed revenue without great friction, and in its original application there was little thought of the relation to national consciousness. But steadily, after 1815, a tariff for revenue was expanded into a protective tariff, and became identified with the ideal of nationality. Clay, the father of the cry for "home markets," sought to popularize his financial policy, by calling it the "American system"—inaccurately differentiating it from a "European system." With the truth or falsity of his financial theories or his terms I have here no concern. The essential thing is that the cry "American system" *was* effective,—that it brought votes, and that it gave to the protection of home industries a support vastly greater than could have been derived from those directly and consciously benefited by protection. The speeches in Congress and on the stump urged protective duties on the score of public revenue, of direct benefit, and of a separate and distinct national ideal, and the last argument usually predominated. The materialistic writer of American history sees in the adoption of a protective system merely the play of industrial interests, nor is it to be denied that these industrial interests were powerful. But the fact must not be lost sight of that the ideal of nation-

ality was used to support the system, that its being
so used is proof of a popular identification of protection with nationality, and above all that when
an industrial interest in 1830, *opposed* to protective
duties, forced a renunciation of the theory of protection, there was brought out the most eloquent
expression yet voiced of a belief in nationality, and
the most determined action yet taken in support
of it.

In 1816 a tariff had been enacted, protective in
its nature, yet intended primarily to raise revenue.
In 1824, after a moderate increase of rates in
various years, the "American system" had come
into its own, and the protective principle was definitely adopted as expressing the "American idea."
And in 1828, partly through the madness of the
protected industries, partly through political chi-
canery on the part of the supporters of Andrew
Jackson's presidential candidacy, there had been
enacted a tariff so high that it was known as the
"Tariff of Abominations,"—so high indeed that
many a man hitherto voting for protection, because
he had been taught to identify it with nationality,
began to question and to doubt.

One section of the United States received little
of the benefit, and felt much of the burden of this
protective system. The South felt that it was
being sacrificed to the rest of the Union, and in
the South there was one man, John C. Calhoun,

so clear of vision that he saw in the growth of the ideal of nationality the loss of the independence of the states,—the loss, as he truly believed, of liberty, for liberty to him meant the freedom of his own state, South Carolina, to guard absolutely her own interests, to control her own destiny. Protection and nationality were identified, then, both by those who supported and those who opposed the protective system. Calhoun struck at protection both in the industrial interests of South Carolina, and to defend her liberty, and the "Tariff of Abominations" gave him his cause and his opportunity. His answer was the famous "Exposition" of Nullification, and the action of his state.

Calhoun's theory of the relation of the states and the federal government rested upon the assumption that the constitution had been adopted by the sovereign states and that these states were still sovereign. The constitution thus viewed as a compact between states, he then asserted that each state, if she considered a law passed by the federal Congress not warranted under the constitution, had a right to declare that law unconstitutional, and to nullify its operation within her own boundaries. This, said Calhoun, is not secession, though it was clearly seen that the "right" of nullification must include ultimately the "right" of secession. But Calhoun's main thesis was the preservation of liberty, and not only the right, but the *duty*, of the

states to preserve their liberty against the encroach-
ments of the nation.   Liberty *versus* Nationality!
This was the essence of the nullification controversy, and when Hayne of South Carolina, speaking in the United States Senate, outlined the theory
of nullification, attacked the protected interests of
the North and especially the selfishness of New
England, threatened that his state would be forced
to action, and pictured her as a *defender of liberty,*
he gave opportunity for passionate expression in
reply of the ideal of nationality.   Webster eagerly
seized the opportunity, and in his famous "Reply to
Hayne," January 26, 1830, sounded the deepest,
most inspiring note of all his oratory.   It was not
a great speech in its logic, in its argument for protection, in its constitutional theory, or even in its
defense of the good name of Massachusetts; its
greatness and its appeal, then and now, rested
wholly in its assertion of the sentiment of nationality, and of a patriotism wider and higher than
mere state patriotism.

"I shall not acknowledge," he said, "that the
honorable member goes before me in regard for
whatever of distinguished talent or distinguished
character South Carolina has produced, I claim
part of the honor, I partake in the pride of her
great names.   I claim them for my countrymen,
one and all, the Laurenses, the Rutledges, the
Pinckneys, the Sumpters, the Marions,—Americans
all, whose fame is no more to be hemmed in by

State lines than their talents and patriotism were capable of being circumscribed within the same narrow limits."

But it was in his peroration that Webster struck the true note of nationality:

"I have not allowed myself, sir, to look beyond the Union to see what might lie hidden in the dark recess behind. I have not coolly weighed the chances of preserving liberty when the bonds that unite us together shall be broken asunder. I have not accustomed myself to hang over the precipice of disunion, to see whether, with my short sight, I can fathom the depth of the abyss below; . . . when my eyes shall be turned to behold for the last time the sun in heaven, may I not see him shining on the broken and dishonored fragments of a once glorious Union; on States dissevered, discordant, belligerent; on a land rent with civil feuds, or drenched, it may be, in fraternal blood! Let their last feeble and lingering glance rather behold the gorgeous ensign of the Republic, now known and honored throughout the earth, still full high advanced, its arms and trophies streaming in their original lustre, not a stripe erased or polluted, not a single star obscured, bearing for its motto no such miserable interrogatory as 'What is all this worth?' nor those other words of delusion and folly, 'Liberty first and Union afterward'; but everywhere, spread all over in characters of living light, blazing on all its ample folds, as they float over the sea and over the land, and in every wind under the whole heavens, that other sentiment, dear to every true American heart,—Liberty *and* Union, now and forever, one and inseparable."

We must not, however, overestimate the immediate effect of, or the general acquiescence in, these stirring words. They were heard with emotion by some, with derision by others, though all felt for the moment the spell of Webster's eloquence. One section of the people applauded either with intense conviction, or from pride in the orator, but another section saw in this speech justification for its fear of a centralized government. It was not until long after Webster's death that North and West were wholly united in the determination to maintain that ideal nationality which Webster had voiced. For the moment indeed there was a feeling, as Benton asserted, that Webster had overstated a crisis, to arouse a popular outcry against South Carolina. But South Carolina was not intimidated. Finding her threats of nullification unheeded, she went on to action, and her legislature prohibited the collection of federal customs dues within her borders. It was then that Andrew Jackson, representing much more truly than did Webster, the opinion of the people of the United States, also expressed his adherence to an ideal of nationality and his determination, as President of the United States, to use force, if necessary, in maintaining that ideal. In a proclamation on December 19, 1832, a comprehensive argument against the theory of nullification, he mingled pleading with threat, but threat was its burden. He asserted the interests of the Union to be superior to the interests of the state, and his language appealed, as he intended it should appeal, to the sentiment of nationality, as something worth fighting for.

"I consider, then," he wrote, "the power to annul a law of the United States, assumed by one State, incompatible with the existence of the Union, contradicted expressly by the letter of the Constitution, unauthorized by its spirit, inconsistent with every principle on which it was founded, and destructive of the great object for which it was formed."

*　　*　　*　　*　　*　　*

"Our Constitution does not contain the absurdity of giving power to make laws, and another power to resist them. . . . The Constitution is still the object of our reverence, the bond of our Union, our defence in danger, the source of our prosperity and peace."

And Jackson notified South Carolina that he would use the forces of the United States to compel obedience to a law of the United States.

The threat was not carried into execution, for there was compromise on the tariff. Clay, the creator of the "American system," but always, first and foremost, a disciple of nationality, yielded his protective principles, and introduced a measure, which gave, as was said, "a lease of nine years to protection, and then the end of that doctrine." Calhoun, claiming this a victory for South Carolina, and yet fearful of Jackson's "ferocity" also, accepted the compromise, but to the end protested that South Carolina had stood for principle—not profit merely. "Disguise it as you may," he said, "the controversy is one between power and liberty," and in that, as he defined the terms, he was absolutely right. But for "power," Webster and Jackson, and all the popular opinion that backed Jackson's threat, read "Nationality,"—and thus reading, gave evidence of their faith in an ideal. That ideal was not yet an universal American faith, but it had found expression as never before in the nullification controversy, and every year added to its strength.

Upon the development of the ideal of nationality for the period between the nullification struggle and the Civil War, I do not dwell, since it was in this period that other ideals, notably those of anti-slavery, and of manifest destiny, topics to be considered in subsequent lectures, more openly held public attention. Yet nationality was inextricably interwoven with both, and the questions of permanent union and of nationality, as opposed by ideals of state liberty, gained steadily in intensity. During this period the South largely imposed its leadership and control upon national policy, and so long as it could do this, was content to let the older issue sleep. With the growth of Northern sentiment against slavery, and of Southern determination to maintain it, there sprang up in the minds of extreme anti-slavery advocates a feeling that the Union, as it stood, was a moral offense, that the North should withdraw from that Union, in short, an anti-nationalistic sentiment. This was the expression, however, of but a few rabid leaders. For a moment, when Texas was annexed, increasing the power of the slave states, and when this was followed by the war with Mexico, even the more moderate of the anti-slavery leaders turned to the idea of separation. Lowell, in the first number of his famous "Biglow Papers," in 1846, expresses it in the lines:

> " Ef I'd *my* way I had ruther
>   We should go to work an' part,
> They take one way, we take t'other,
>   Guess it wouldn't break my heart;"

But this feeling did not last, and in his later "Biglow Papers," he quickly changed the note, using his genius in a sharp arraignment of Southern ideals, especially of the asserted benefits of slavery to the slave, as well as in attack upon the injustice to Mexico of the war. The personal note in these poems is one of almost bitter despair and pessimism, yet in the end he reasserted in possibly his most famous lines, his faith in the ultimate triumph of high principles and ideals.

> " Truth forever on the scaffold, Wrong forever on the
>   throne;
>   Yet that scaffold sways the future, and behind the dim
>   unknown
>   Standeth God within the shadow, keeping watch above
>   his own."

It is, however, in the Civil War that this ideal of nationality at last asserted itself as the most powerful influence in all our history. Before that fratricidal struggle had actually begun, there were many in the North who, with sorrow for the impending separation, yet nevertheless could not tolerate the thought of an appeal to arms to preserve the Union. Oliver Wendell Holmes, in a "Lament for Sister Caroline," wrote:

> " Go, then, our rash sister, afar and aloof,—
>   Run wild in the sunshine away from our roof;
>   But when your heart aches and your feet have grown
>   sore,
>   Remember the pathway that leads to our door!"

But even in these lines Holmes reveals his faith in the ultimate victory of the nationalistic ideal, and when the news came of the attack on Fort Sumter, he, with all who had doubted, was suddenly transformed into an ardent patriot, ready, if need be, to sacrifice his all for the preservation of the Union. The memoirs and autobiographies of that day, one and all, bear witness to the marvelous change that took place in the sentiments of the North, when the news came from Charleston. From the time of the election of Lincoln, in November, 1860, to the attack on Sumter, all had been doubt, confusion, uncertainty, even regret for Lincoln's victory at the polls. Suddenly this atmosphere of pessimism and dismay was cleared away by a specific act, raising a specific question,—the question of preserving the Union,—of preserving the ideal of nationality.

It has been my good fortune while at Yale to secure from Professor Lounsbury a statement of his experiences in New York City in 1861, a portion of which I here present as illustrating this sudden change in sentiment. Professor Lounsbury writes:

"During the months of January and February, as I remember, Booth was playing at the old Winter Garden theater. One piece he frequently acted was Richelieu. That I went to hear one evening in the early part of February. In it occurs a passage in which Richelieu is represented as saying:

> 'Take away the sword.
> States can be saved without it.'

As this was uttered the audience went into a transport of enthusiasm. Not merely was there a thunder of applause, but hats were thrown into the air, and individuals might be said to have almost screamed with excitement and enthusiasm. Every one was thinking of the differences that then prevailed and the controversies that were going on, and the audience was proclaiming its hostility to any suggestion of war between the two sections. Booth gave up his engagements at the theater for the time being, but sometime in April, I think, returned to it to begin another. It was during this second engagement that the attack on Fort Sumter was made. I again went to hear him. When it came to the passage previously welcomed with such thunderous applause, there was preserved a dead silence. It passed without notice. But in the previous act there was a conversation between Richelieu and his confidant, the Capuchin Joseph. In that, words were spoken which the first time I heard the play had been received in silence. Richelieu had been represented as saying:

> 'First employ
> All methods to conciliate.'

" 'Failing then?' inquires Joseph. To this Richelieu answers fiercely, 'All means to crush.' This passage was now hailed with a tremendous uproar. The same scene was enacted as had taken place at the previous representation, when the other passage had been spoken, and this time with even a more tempestuous welcome."

Another description of this marvelous change in Northern sentiment is that given by Carl Schurz.

He had just returned from Washington to Wisconsin, when the news came of the attack on Fort Sumter, and of the President's call for volunteers. Schurz hastened back to Washington. Of this journey he writes:

"When only a short time before I had traveled from Washington westward, a dreadful gloom of expectancy seemed to oppress the whole country. Passengers in the railway cars talked together in murmurs, as if afraid of the sound of their own voices. At the railroad stations stood men with anxious faces waiting for the newspapers, which they hastily opened to read the headings, and then handed the papers to another with sighs of disappointment. Multitudes of people seemed to be perplexed not only as to what they might expect, but also as to what they wished. And now what a change! Every railroad station filled with an excited crowd hurrahing for the Union and Lincoln. The Stars and Stripes fluttering from numberless staffs.

"It is impossible to describe the electric effect these occurrences produced upon the popular mind in the Northern States. Until the first gun was fired upon Fort Sumter many patriotic people still entertained a lingering hope of saving the Union without a conflict of arms. Now civil war had suddenly become a certainty. The question of what might have been utterly vanished before the question of what was to be. A mighty shout arose that the Republic must be saved at any cost. It was one of those sublime moments of patriotic exaltation when everybody seems willing to do everything and to sacrifice everything for a common cause—one of those ideal sun-bursts in the history of nations."*

Let me cite still another observer, of cooler temperament, and more philosophic mind. I quote the words of Emerson:

"At the darkest hour in the history of the republic, when it looked as if the nation would be dismembered, pulverized into its original elements, the attack on Fort Sumter chrystallized the North into a unit, and the hope of mankind was saved."

What was this force that could "chrystallize" a people, could make it a unit in action? Was it a fear of industrial benefit about to be lost? or the assertion of economic principles? or a belief in the evils of slavery? or a conviction on a theory of the constitution? It was none of these. Rather a blow struck at the emblem of an ideal had suddenly revealed to a troubled people the place that ideal held in their hearts. The issue was clear at last, the long days of anxious waiting were over, and everywhere, in all parties and all factions, there was felt the *will* to preserve the Union. Other objects were forgotten, constitutional argument was ignored, and simply the sense of country, of nationality, rose supreme.

* These paragraphs are in inverse order in Schurz, Reminiscences II, 223-224.

As the war progressed, other ideals and objects came to be expressed also, but throughout, the ideal of nationality was the dominant one in the North. Very early in the struggle those who had stood for the cause of anti-slavery believed that the war would not end without the extinction of that hated system. Lowell, who at the opening of the Mexican War, had doubted the permanence of the Union, now wrote, January 6, 1862, in a new series of the "Biglow Papers," his poem entitled "Jonathan to John," addressed indeed to Great Britain, and expressing America's resentment of British action in the *Trent* affair, but concluding with lines expressing his faith in nationality and in ideals triumphant.

> " God means to make this land, John,
>   Clear thru, from sea to sea,
> Believe an' understand, John,
>   The *wuth* o' bein' free.
>   Ole Uncle S. sez he, 'I guess
>   God's price is high,' sez he;
> 'But nothin' else than wut he sells
>   Wears long, an' thet J. B.
>   May larn, like you an' me!'"

This was a prediction of emancipation. Julia Ward Howe tells us in her recollections, that, visiting Washington, she was distressed to find the soldiers singing the doggerel of "John Brown's Body," and wishing to provide words for the music, more suitable and more inspiring, wrote the "Battle Hymn of the Republic." That poem, as Kipling has well said, is a "terrible" one. It is filled with the wrath of God, and the joy of self-sacrifice, while in the line,

" As He died to make men holy, let us die to make men free,"

the author stated *her* conception of the object of the war.

Nor was Mrs. Howe the only writer who sought to replace the words of the soldiers' song with lines more refined and, as it was thought, more suitable to the conflict. Edna Dean Proctor attempted this in the poem, "John Brown," suited to the rhythm of the song:

" John Brown died on the scaffold for the slave;
   Dark was the hour when we dug his hallowed grave;
   Now God avenges the life he gladly gave,
       Freedom reigns today !"

All three of these poems were written before Lincoln's emancipation proclamation had been issued, but, in spite of the hopes of their authors, the latter two were not sung by the Northern armies. The "Battle Hymn of the Republic," an expression of real genius and intense feeling, then, as now, aroused the emotions, but the testimony of the soldiers themselves is that they sang "John Brown's Body" for its marching swing and for its sentiment, and it is to be noted that, as originally sung, it contained no reference to the slave, except the repetition of the name, "John Brown." In fact, the verses emphatically preferred by the soldier in the ranks, were:

" They'll hang Jeff Davis on a sour apple tree,"

and

" Now for the Union let's give three rousing cheers."

These lines really expressed to the army the ideal for which it was fighting, and in them were bitterness toward those who would disrupt the Union, as well as determination to save it.

It was Lincoln, however, who with that pith and brevity in which he had no equal, best expressed the ideal of nationality, paramount to all other ideals in this conflict. By the summer of 1862 it had become clear that the dream of a short war was but a dream. Anti-slavery sentiment in the North gained strength, partly from conviction, partly from a desire to punish the South, partly from a belief in emancipation as a necessary war measure. Horace Greeley, the influential editor of the *New York Tribune*, addressed an editorial to Lincoln, naming it "The Prayer of 20,000,000

People," and urging the issue of an edict of emancipation. Lincoln wrote and made public a reply. After waiving discussion of many misstatements in Greeley's "Prayer," he said:

"If there be those who would not save the Union, unless they could at the same time save slavery, I do not agree with them.

"If there be those who would not save the Union, unless they could at the same time destroy slavery, I do not agree with them.

"My paramount object is to save the Union, and not either to save or destroy slavery.

"If I could save the Union without freeing any slaves, I would do it. And if I could save it by freeing all the slaves, I would do it. And if I could save it by freeing some, and leaving others alone, I would also do that.

"What I do about slavery and the colored race, I do because I believe it helps to save the Union, and what I forbear, I forbear, because I do not believe it would help save the Union."

At the moment when Lincoln wrote these words, so truly representative of the will of the people, there was lying in his desk the draft of the Emancipation Proclamation, to be issued if, in the exigencies of war, it should seem wise to issue it, as a war measure. The liberty of the slaves appealed to the "great emancipator," but far higher was the appeal of nationality.

The ideal of unity, of nationality, was not con-

fined to the North.   The Civil War has been
depicted as a contest between the ideals of national
unity and state liberty, and in its inception and
theoretical basis this is no doubt true.   Lee's personal struggle, his self-examination, as to where
duty lay, was typical of the reasoned, not merely
the emotional forces, that led men to stand by their
states.   But the conflict had barely begun when,
by the requirements of war, state liberty, even in
the Confederacy, had to yield to national unity, and
this ideal of a Southern unity found expression in
the literature of the South.   In Albert Pike's poem,
"Dixie," there is no note of the liberty of the state.
The very first verse is a call to country:

> " Southrons, hear your country call you!
> Up, lest worse than death befall you!
>   To arms! To arms! To arms, in Dixie!
> Lo! all the beacon-fires are lighted,—
> Let all hearts be now united!
>   To arms! To arms! To arms! in Dixie!
>   Advance the flag of Dixie!
> For Dixie's land we take our stand,
>   And live and die for Dixie!"

and faith in divine guidance was not wanting either,
as in the verse:

> " Swear upon your country's altar
>   Never to submit or falter,
>   Till the spoilers are defeated,
>   Till the Lord's work is completed!"

It is a remarkable fact that in the earlier period of the war, while at the North there existed, and was much expression of, intense bitterness, and soon of a desire to punish the South for forcing the conflict, in the South, neither statesman nor poet gave voice to sentiments of revenge. This may have been due to a conviction of victory bred in the South, or possibly to an underlying sentiment of regret that she had been compelled to strike a blow at the "once glorious Union." But as the war dragged on, and the issue became more doubtful for the independence of a Southern nation,—when indeed the South began to suffer, then came the expression of a desire to inflict suffering. Henry Timrod, in the "Cotton Boll," a dreamy contemplation of the virtues of cotton production, and its many blessings, suddenly turns, toward the close of his poem, to a fervent appeal for divine aid in avenging the South as a nation:

" Oh, help us, Lord! to roll the crimson flood
  Back on its course, and, while our banners wing
  Northward, strike with us! till the Goth shall cling
  To his own blasted altar-stones, and crave
  Mercy; and we shall grant it, and dictate
  The lenient future of his fate
  There, where some rolling ships and crumbling quays
  Shall one day mark the Port which ruled the Western
      seas."

The Civil War began indeed, as Calhoun had

feared, in a conflict between "power and liberty," nationality and states' rights. The result of the war settled for all time that question. The ideal of nationality triumphed because it had back of it a superior material force,—an argument of the materialistic historian,—but that force could never have been exerted had it not been for a united idealization of nationality. In the later ready acceptance of that same ideal by the South, is to be read in the South itself, even throughout the struggle, perhaps even renewed by the struggle, a subconscious acceptance of the binding power of the ideal of nationality. In times of national danger, genius in literary expression finds inspiration in patriotism. The popular approval of such expressions is one evidence, and an important one, of a nation's faith. During the Civil War Edward Everett Hale wrote that wonderful story, "The Man Without a Country," and it at once held the hearts of the North as did no other writing of the time. But more recently, in the Spanish-American War, and since, that story has been reprinted, especially in the South, and read again and again, as if it were new, as indeed it always will be new to American hearts. It is simply a confession of faith in the ideal of nationality. In concluding this lecture, permit me then to recall the narrative and quote the closing paragraph.

The hero of the story is Philip Nolan, a young

army officer stationed in the West at the beginning
of the nineteenth century, who falls a victim to the
magnetism of Aaron Burr, joins the supposed plan
for a new western empire, and forgets his duty and
his loyalty to his native land.   While being tried
for treason in 1807 Nolan, angered by some question of the presiding judge, "cried out in a fit of
frenzy, 'Damn the United States! I wish I may
never hear of the United States again.'"   The old
judge was shocked beyond expression, and when
Nolan was convicted, condemned him to the literal
execution of his own wish, "never to hear the name
of the United States again."   He was placed as a
perpetual prisoner on board a United States naval
vessel, officers and crew were instructed to treat
him kindly, but were never to mention to him, or
to permit him information about, the United States,
and as he was transferred from vessel to vessel,
these same orders were enforced, though Nolan,
at first defiant, soon sought, by entreaty, stratagem,
or bribes, to be told something of his country, but
all in vain.   Thus situated, he went through the
war of 1812, cruised many times about the globe
but was never permitted to enter an American
port, passed through the Mexican War, found new
faces always, grew old, his story almost forgotten,
while naval commanders, in the cradle when he was
condemned, continued to carry out the instructions
of 1807.   At last, during the Civil War, on May 11,

1863, dying, he excited the compassion of Captain Danforth, who commanded the vessel on which Nolan then was, and Danforth visited Nolan in his stateroom, yielded to his entreaties and poured into his eager ears the story of his country's history,— of the war of 1812, of the acquisition of Florida, of Texas and California, and of Oregon. Danforth told him of industries, of railroads, and of cities; of books, and colleges, of West Point and the Naval School. Together the two drew in, upon a map that Nolan had long since constructed in vague and uncertain outline, seventeen new states added to the Union since Nolan had been condemned never again to hear of his country.

"And," says Danforth, "he drank it in, and enjoyed it as I cannot tell you. He grew more and more silent, yet I never thought he was tired or faint. I gave him a glass of water, but he just wet his lips, and told me not to go away. Then he asked me to bring the Presbyterian 'Book of Public Prayer,' which lay there, and said with a smile, that it would open at the right place,—and so it did. There was his double red mark down the page; and I knelt down and read, and he repeated with me: 'For ourselves and our country, O gracious God, we thank thee that notwithstanding our manifold transgressions of thy holy laws, thou hast continued to us thy marvelous kindness,'—and so to the end of that thanksgiving. Then he turned to the end of the same book, and I read the words more familiar to me: 'Most heartily we beseech thee with thy favor to behold and bless thy servant the President of the United States, and all others in authority,'—and the rest of the Episcopal collect. 'Danforth,' said he, 'I have repeated those prayers night and morning, it is now fifty-five years.' And then he said he would go to sleep. . . . And I went away."

II

ANTI-SLAVERY—A CRUSADE

ANTI-SLAVERY—A CRUSADE

It is now generally conceded that while anti-slavery attracted attention and discussion previous to 1860, it had no such hold on the people as to preclude other interests, and that its influence in bringing on the war has been overestimated. Immediately after the Civil War, indeed, popular retrospect pictured the North as long in the grip of anti-slavery sentiment, and men were prone to think of themselves as animated in 1850 by the same ideals they later held in 1865. Modern historians have corrected this error, but today the correction has itself assumed the proportions of an error. Instead of a just estimate of the real influence of the anti-slavery movement, we have now a tendency to deny both its actual extent, and its force as an ideal. Recently, at the American Historical Association in Boston, 1912, one of the speakers affirmed his belief that careful investigation of church history between 1840 and 1860 would show that the general sentiment of church members and church organizations in the North was definitely inimical to the anti-slavery movement, thus denying its force as an ideal in religious bodies. An able student of history in its geographic conditions has written as follows:

"The morale of the institution [slavery] like the right of secession, was long a mooted question, until New England, having discovered the economic un-fitness of slave industry to her boulder-strewn soil, took the lead in the crusade against it."

Here is no denial that anti-slavery *was* an ideal and a force, but the inception of that ideal is found in geographic environment. An economic historian, in a chapter entitled "Why the Civil War came," goes much farther than most writers. He states that the causes of the war were not "found either in the wickedness of chattel slavery, nor in the growing moral consciousness of the North. . . . It is certain that the general moral conscience of the North had seldom been lower than in the years when competitive capitalism [1840 to 1860] was gaining the mastery in American industrial life."

These citations are sufficient to indicate the pres-ent tendency to minimize in our history the force of the anti-slavery ideal, or to deny its spiritual vigor. I believe these interpretations, or explana-tions, to be true only in part, that these were con-tributing rather than conclusive causes, and that back of the sordid, tangible explanation was an inspiring sentiment that touched men's hearts and fired imagination. In support of my contention, I wish to present to you, as before, a few quotations illustrative of the origin, growth, and influence of the anti-slavery ideal.

Historically considered, I believe that opposition to slavery among Christian nations had its origin in the teachings of Christ, and that when men's minds turned from theological dogma to consider life and service, there emerged an antagonism to slavery. In America, it was in fact exactly in those religious communities where the brotherhood of man was most insisted on that anti-slavery sentiment first appeared. This was among the Quakers and in pre-revolutionary times. African slavery existed in all the American colonies, and it can not be said that in colonial times there was any general feeling against it. But when the doctrines of the Declaration of Independence, as understood by the majority of men, came to reinforce religious hostility, there immediately sprang up a number of definitely organized anti-slavery societies. By 1827 slavery had been abolished in all the Northern states, while societies for the further expansion of the movement had been organized in every state in the Union, except in the extreme South, in Indiana, and in New England.

This earlier movement was largely moral and religious. Its chief center of activity and its chief support were in the so-called border states, especially in Kentucky and in Virginia, and here the

conviction existed that slavery was a moral evil.
Previous to 1830 the great advocate of emancipation was a Quaker, Benjamin Lundy, who traveled
freely though the South, and was kindly received.
But between 1827 and 1830 the movement gradually lost its hold upon the people. This rapid
decay of a campaign of ideals, has always excited
the wonder of the historian, and various reasons
have been asserted for it,—reasons which I may
not pause to examine, but it is worthy of notice
that in the whole civilized world the period of the
late twenties was one of apathy to ideals.   In
Europe this was manifested in political reaction
against the ideals of the French Revolution,—in
the loss of younger enthusiasms,—a moral stagna-
tion not recovered from till the revolutions of 1830,
which had their origin in a remembrance of the
things that were *good* in the revolution of 1789.
In America the same wave, or germ, call it what
you will, of intellectual and spiritual unrest, expressed itself in various forms, one of which was
the new abolition movement initiated by William
Lloyd Garrison.

Garrisonian abolition may be traced in part to
the older movement, but it also differed materially
from it. While the earlier agitation urged emancipation for slaves, based upon religious conviction,
the new gospel *demanded* freedom for slaves upon
all grounds, moral, social, and political.   In place

of an ethical question came a positive command. Denunciation was substituted for moral suasion. "Thou shalt not" displaced the older "it is better not." The new gospel proclaimed that the nation, if it would save its soul, must not hold slaves. Garrison placarded slavery as a damnable wrong, and slave owners as doomed to damnation, unless they forswore slavery, while the Northerner was first appealed to to join in placing this stigma upon slavery, and refusing, was condemned as *particeps criminis*. Not all anti-slavery leaders held such extreme views, yet from the first the movement assumed the proportions of a moral crusade, and its converts were impelled by an ideal. Let us examine its expressions, and estimate their actual influence.

Convinced that Lundy's milder methods had been ineffective and useless, Garrison in 1830 came to Boston and established the *Liberator*. In the first issue of that paper he stated his purpose:

"I shall strenuously contend for the immediate enfranchisement of our slave population. . . . I am aware that many object to the severity of my language; but is there not cause for severity? I *will* be as harsh as truth, and as uncompromising as justice. On this subject, I do not wish to think, or speak, or write, with moderation. I am in earnest—I will not equivocate—I will not retreat a single inch—and I will be heard."

The *Liberator* became, then, the organ of the cause, and its editor the chief apostle. Garrison was a trenchant writer and a vigorous fighter. His demand, throughout his entire career, was for immediate and absolute emancipation, ignoring all practical difficulties, depicting and exaggerating the horrors of slavery, and seeking to create a universal will in the free states for a national casting off of slavery as a national sin. He recognized no distinction in the owners of slaves, lashing all alike in virulent language. He asserted that the need of the hour was to convert the North, to arouse it and create a powerful sentiment so strong that force, presumably political, would be used to compel the South to free its slaves.

The immediate response to Garrison's appeal gave evidence of the existence of an intense feeling, hitherto unsuspected, in the North. Anti-slavery societies sprang rapidly into existence. By 1832 there were so many societies in New England that a federation was established. In 1833 the "American Society" was organized in Philadelphia and the spread of local societies throughout the North was extremely rapid. In 1835 there were two hundred of them, in 1836 five hundred, and by 1840 two thousand, nearly all well financed and prosperous, with a total membership of 175,000. Radical and denunciatory, the movement at first repelled rather than attracted men of power and reputation. Later the appeal overshadowed the manner and method, and such men as Whittier and Wendell Phillips came to its aid. Whittier's service as speaker and writer was valuable, but his most effective weapon was found in his poems. Wendell Phillips as an orator gifted in invective, never checked by facts, wholly intolerant, made use of the public platform, as Garrison used the press. Later came Theodore Parker in the pulpit, James Russell Lowell in prose and poetry, Palfrey in history. In the West there was immediate evidence of the moral appeal of anti-slavery to the youth of the nation. At Lane Theological Seminary, in Cincinnati, under the presidency of Lyman Beecher, a student debate on the question of slavery resulted in an expression of abolition sentiment. The Seminary drew from both banks of the Ohio, and the trustees, fearing to lose Southern students, prohibited public discussions of slavery. Nearly four fifths of the students withdrew to Oberlin College. Thus was created the Oberlin anti-slavery movement, furnishing a center for the agitation in the West. In the North as a whole there were three general groups. New England gave to the cause writers and orators, working on purely theoretical lines. The Middle States financed the movement, which drew support from the resources of wealthy philanthropists. The West attempted more practical operations, offering education to free negroes, and beginning that systematized aid to escaping slaves which later was known as the Underground Railroad. In all sections the membership of the societies was largely composed of young men.

By 1835 anti-slavery had become a well-organized, definite propaganda, and from being derided had come to be feared and hated. The conservative and peace-seeking elements in the North, at first indifferent, were roused to forcible opposition. Garrison himself made the opening, for, driven by opposition to defend his crusade in all its aspects, and disappointed that he failed to arouse co-operation in the churches, he charged his impotence upon the church and the patriotic sense of the people. Such attitude could only be abhorrent to the great masses, and particularly so to two great ideal forces in America,—religion and patriotism. Smarting under church opposition, he renounced attendance in the Baptist church, proclaimed his disbelief in the inspiration of the Bible, denied the authority of tradition and inspiration, and ended by founding all his convictions on the philosophical basis of "natural right" and "reason." Inevitably the cry of infidelity was raised against anti-slavery. In addition he unhesitatingly advocated Northern secession as the only measure left when the cause was politically ignored. To the horror of sincere patriots he called the constitution "a covenant with death and an agreement with hell." Though this was but a temporary attitude, it alarmed his adherents and gave to conservatism its opportunity. For a moment even Whittier doubted, but in the end he declared for the utmost free expression of abolition doctrines, writing

"If we have whispered truth, whisper no longer,
  Speak as the trumpet does,—sterner and stronger."

The attack on Garrisonian abolition came from every element of society. Evidence of church opposition is found in the New England Pastoral letter of 1837 to the Congregational churches, condemning discussion of abolition in the pulpit, as certain to disrupt the church. A noted preacher, Prof. Moses Stuart of Andover Theological Seminary, found justification for slavery in the New Testament. In 1836 the Methodist Conference of New York State censured two of its members for favoring abolition. Such clerical intolerance but aroused the anti-slavery leaders to greater vigor. In a poem entitled "Clerical Oppressors," Whittier wrote:

"Just God! and these are they
  Who minister at thine altar, God of Right!
  Men who their hands with prayer and blessing lay
  On Israel's Ark of light!"

   *   *   *   *   *   *   *

"Feed fat, ye locusts, feed!
  And, in your tasseled pulpits, thank the Lord

That, from the toiling bondsman's utter need,
Ye pile your own full board.

" How long, O Lord! how long
Shall such a priesthood barter truth away,
And in Thy name, for robbery and wrong
At Thy own altars pray?"

In institutions of learning also the controversy
raged, always with the few on the side of anti-
slavery, and the many against it.   Prof. Charles
Follen was dropped from the Harvard faculty as
too open in his advocacy of the cause.   In New
Haven a plan to establish a manual training school
for negroes was opposed by the town authorities,
for fear it would endanger the popularity of Yale
College.   In 1832 Miss Crandall admitted a negress
to her girls' school at Canterbury, Connecticut,
whereupon the white scholars left.   Miss Crandall
then advertised a colored school.   The town
objected and arrested her pupils as vagrants.   They
were bailed out and returned to school.   The legislature passed an act prohibiting the school.   Miss
Crandall defied the law, was arrested, and later
freed by the Supreme Court of the state.   Then
there followed a combined boycott by the shop-
keepers, physicians, and ministers of the surround-
ing community, and the school was forced to close.
At Phillips Andover Academy a situation developed
of unusual interest, though, so far as I am aware,

it has attracted little attention from the historians of anti-slavery. My knowledge of it comes from the unpublished diaries and letters of one who took part in it. Garrison, thinking to make use of English enthusiasm for the cause, had invited to America a noted speaker, George Thompson. Let an old man of eighty-six tell in his own language the effect of Thompson's lectures upon a boy of sixteen in Phillips Academy.

"In the summer of 1835 Thompson came to Andover and gave eleven lectures in a small Methodist church, the only church that could be obtained for him, yet it was large enough for those who would go to hear such doctrine. There was with him one of our ministers by the name of Phelps, who afterwards wrote a book called 'Phelps on Slavery.' They had with them a young darkey who had run away from his master and whom, after they had had their say, they trotted out to tell a little about his slave life and how he had escaped from it, which he did with a glib tongue and forceful effect. I, with many of the students not only of the Academy but a number of those in the Theological Seminary, attended the lectures. For the proposition to form an anti-slavery society I had a ready assent, not simply because of the influence of the lectures but because from earlier influences I was already an abolitionist. So it was that by a previous training set on fire by the eloquence of Thompson in his Andover lectures, for he was an eloquent man, I was ready to join an anti-slavery society.

I was one of fifty or sixty others that were ready for the same. The teachers and trustees felt that the formation of such a society would be a disgrace and an injury to the popularity of the school and of course were opposed to it. Still claiming, in spite of their opposition, what seemed to us a right and duty for us to do, we were counted as rebels and begun to be treated as such. The first step was to deprive us of the privilege of recitation. One of our number drew up a statement of what we conceived to be our principles, rights, etc., to be presented to the public. We went out into the woods (or the timber as Westerners have it) to hear the address and consider. We endorsed the statement and solemnly pledged to stand together in contending for our rights and principles. Soon at morning prayers came this announcement to us all: 'Those of age must return to their studies within three days as loyal students or be expelled from the institution. All minors are to return at once. You in a sense are by your parents committed to our charge and we enjoin upon you what in our judgment they would have you do.' This in effect. Before leaving the room I went directly to the principal (Mr. Osgood) remonstrating. 'I can't,' he said, 'I can't do otherwise. I am bound as in chains.' 'But,' I said, 'I do not know what my parents would have me do, nor do you. May I have leave to go and see?' 'Yes,' said he, 'go home for three days. You will cool off and be prepared to come back.' I went home. When evening came, I told my father the whole story, at the close saying, 'Now, father, I will go back or not, just as you say.' He said nothing, except, 'Well, you may go to bed now.' The next morning he said nothing till about ten o'clock when the sun had dried up the dew; he simply said, 'Well, my son, you may take the fork and open the haycocks today.' That was all he said, or ever said, about it. I went to work and worked with a will, glad that I was free from Phillips Academy, and that I had brought all my books with me, for I knew well enough what Father meant."

Of the boys who took part in this "Andover Rebellion," and who later attended college, the majority went to Dartmouth, having been discouraged from making application to other colleges of New England. The incident is a striking illustration of the appeal to youth made by the ideals of anti-slavery, and in this case is all the more remarkable in that the students of the Theological Seminary did not approve the cause, and even tried to break up Thompson's meetings. The bringing of Thompson to America was indeed a blunder. The American people were peculiarly sensitive to "English interference," and their resentment was food for Garrison's opponents. There followed the Boston riot of October 21, 1835, from which Thompson fled, and in which Garrison was led through the streets with a halter about his neck. The handbill, which was distributed in the city and which led to the riot, reveals both the intensity of feeling, and its causes.

THOMPSON

The Abolitionist.

That infamous foreign scoundrel *Thompson* will hold forth *this afternoon,* at the Liberator Office, No. 48 Washington Street. The present is a fair opportunity for the friends of the Union, to *smoke Thompson out!* It will be a contest between the Abolitionists and the friends of the Union. A purse of $100 has been raised by a number of patriotic citizens to reward the individual who shall first lay violent hands on Thompson, so that he may be brought to the tar kettle before dark. Friends of the Union be vigilant!

Boston, Wednesday, 12 o'clock.

The year 1836 marks the end of this first "stormy" period of the anti-slavery crusade. Thereafter Garrison and his friends abandoned violent measures and methods. Abuse gave place to moderation and the following was increased. Yet the accession of men of note was slow. Emerson, a real friend of anti-slavery, cringed before the intemperate language of some of its leaders. "Let us," he wrote, "withhold every reproachful, and, if we can, every indignant remark. In this cause, we must renounce our temper, and the risings of pride." He would, he said, "convince" the slave owner that it was "cheaper to pay wages than to own slaves." It is customarily stated that the intelligent conservative opposition to Garrison in New England rested on respect for property, respect for the constitution as a bargain made, and fear of black atrocities such as had taken place in San Domingo. This classification omits the leading commercial interest vested in the cotton mills, and voiced in State Street. The whole conservative tradition of wealth, intelligence, blood, and political control was against anti-slavery. Its leaders were negligible, but the ideal was greater than the leaders, and in the next two decades many a natural conservative was drawn, almost in spite of himself, into the cause of anti-slavery. And there was yet another element of strength in the movement. At first opposed by patriotic sentiment that feared its influence in severing the nation, it later found support in the North from the very ideal of nationality,—an ideal that clung not merely to union, but to a union devoted to moral principles. Had political conceptions remained fixed as before 1815, there would have been no Northern outcry against slavery in the old states of the South, and little against its expansion to the West. The mere growth of anti-slavery in its later aspect is an evidence of the spread of the sentiment of nationality.

It is in the South, however, that we may trace the more positive effects of the anti-slavery ideal.

The earlier attitude of the South had been friendly to theories of emancipation, but puzzled in regard to the practical application of those theories. But the South resented Northern criticism. Benton, as late as 1830, reflected the older opinion, stating "slavery, in the abstract has but few advocates, or defenders, in the slave holdings states, and . . . it would have fewer advocates among us than it has, if those who have nothing to do with the subject, would only let us alone." Under the irritation of the anti-slavery oratory, observing the growth of the anti-slavery societies, Southern leaders were driven to a defense of the morality of slavery. Governor McDuffie of South Carolina, in the middle thirties, was the first official champion of this new attitude. In a message to the legislature, he asserted that democracy meant a democracy of the intelligent merely, and that this was possible only where a servile labor class offered to the intelligent, opportunity and freedom to exercise their duties as citizens. Slavery, he claimed, was the essential bulwark of democracy; and the Bible was cited to prove the sanctity of the institution as directly ordered in the scheme of divine providence. McDuffie was in advance of most of the South, and his message was severely criticised, but by 1850 the South was practically a unit in supporting these ideas, everywhere spread by press and pulpit. Opposition and attack naturally unify the elements in defense. Anti-slavery agitation created pro-slavery harmony in ideals,—forced the adoption of those ideals for which Southerners were ready to sacrifice their all. Southern resentment of the jeers of this band of idealists culminated in an effort to prohibit the discussion of slavery in the halls of Congress. There followed the famous battle of John Quincy Adams, for the right of petition. The contest lasted for years. In 1838, in a debate on the proposed annexation of Texas, Adams introduced a petition against annexation, on the ground of slavery, and then attempted to debate the question from this point of view. Instantly he was called to order by the speaker, Polk, who stated that slavery was not under discussion,—as if any condition in a state whose annexation was under discussion were not debatable. The House supported Polk's ruling, evidence of the illogical lengths to which the South and its Northern allies would go to prevent expression of anti-slavery sentiment. Yet in this same debate, Campbell of South Carolina was permitted to *defend* slavery, stating that while there had been of old in the South a fear that it might be, perhaps, morally wrong, Northern criticism had led the South to a careful investigation which "has satisfied all sound minds that slavery is neither a moral nor a political evil . . . it has relieved many minds from very painful and uneasy feelings." John Quincy Adams was no abolitionist, but he was an eager fighter, and when, in these contests, he heard the North constantly threatened with a Southern secession, he answered, "Let it come; if it must come in blood, yet I say let it come."

I have no intention of dilating upon the arguments for and against slavery,—rather my purpose is to show by incident and quotation the intensity of feeling, the real conviction, aroused by the anti-slavery ideal,—to prove its constant influence on our history from 1830 through the Civil War, and even after. It welded the South into a unit, firm in defense of the institution in the old states, seeking expansion and power in new states, and ultimately turning to the theory of state liberty as the only salvation. In the North the movement gained power as the South became more arrogant in defiance. The Southerners' favorite comparison of the lot of the slaves with that of the poor of Great Britain, was met by Channing's retort, "Misery is not slavery." In the forties, the proposed annexation of Texas drove hundreds of the more intelligent of New England into the ranks of the abolitionists. The older leaders, formerly despised, became popular. Phillips could even jeer at the constitution, telling the conservative "Union" men to "say the constitution backwards instead of your prayers, and there will be no rebellion." Garrison was more happy and more convincing, when, on July 4, he spoke on "The Lessons of Independence Day," and said:

"I present myself as the advocate of my enslaved countrymen, at a time when their claim cannot be shuffled out of sight, and on an occasion which entitles me to a respectful hearing in their behalf. If I am asked to prove their title to liberty, my answer is, that the fourth of July is not a day to be wasted in establishing 'self-evident truths.'"

The Mexican War was heart-breaking to the anti-slavery leaders, who saw its inception in a determination to expand slave territory and fix the institution for all time on the American nation. Momentarily, weariness and dismay caused a desire to separate from the South. Whittier wrote:

> "Take your land of sun and bloom;
> Only leave to Freedom room
> For her plough, and forge, and loom;"

but soon with restored courage and a renewed faith in the future of this nation, the contest assumed wider proportions, and this largely because of the new men who now joined it. Such men as Burlingame, Wilson, Sumner, Dana, Palfrey, Charles Francis Adams, Mann, Chase, and Hale, all of whom earlier were at least indifferent, came to swell the list of influential workers. Lowell was a tower of strength, especially in his "Biglow

Papers." He stated the "Pious Editor's Creed" in these words:

> " I du believe in Freedom's cause,
>   Ez fur away ez Payris is;
> I love to see her stick her claws
>   In them infarnal Phayrisees;
> It's wal enough agin a king
>   To dror resolves an' triggers,—
> But libbaty's a kind o' thing
>   Thet don't agree with niggers."

Labored economic contentions to prove the inefficiency of slave as compared with free labor, were not wanting either. But the Southern answer to this was easy,—as that of Governor Hammond, who admitted the economic superiority of free labor, and continued:

"But the question is whether free or slave labor is cheapest to us in this country, *at this time, situated as we are*. And it is to be decided at once by the fact that we cannot avail ourselves of any other than slave labor."

and this conviction, unquestionably sincere, intensified Southern belief in the rightfulness of slavery.

After the annexations of the Mexican War,— when California was admitted as a free state, when the Compromise of 1850 had apparently settled for all the territory of the Union the conditions and extent of slavery, there was a distinct reaction in the intensity of this conflict of ideals, and on both sides. Except among a few extremists, the dominant note was one of thankfulness for danger escaped, and determination, for the safety of the Union, to avoid disturbing comments. This was what was meant by the "finality" of the compromise. In both North and South the elder statesmen, intensely loyal to the Union, seeing it threatened by slavery agitation, urged "finality" and sought to quiet all discussion,—dilating upon the trade relations of the two sections. A few of the younger, or newer, men were not content. Jefferson Davis led the extreme faction of the South, while Seward became the champion of Northern idealists, asserting "Whoever declares that trade is the cement of this Union, libels the idea of American civilization." The trend of public sentiment seemed, however, to be toward conciliation, until Douglas of Illinois, with no conception of the deep underlying feeling of the North, aroused Northern wrath by his bill for the Kansas-Nebraska territory. That bill provided for the territory of Kansas, with or without slavery, as the people of the territory might elect. "We are betrayed," shouted the anti-slavery leaders, and the people, sincerely believing in the finality of the legislation of 1850, considering themselves tricked, responded to the cry with a frenzy that astounded Douglas, and stirred an answering challenge from the South. The bill was passed in May, 1854, and slaveholders from Missouri at once crossed into the new territory. A cry went up in the North for an emigration of free labor, to "save Kansas," and already there was organized in New England the Emigrant Aid Society, whose first party started for Kansas in July, 1854, led by strong men and vigorous fighters. To them Whittier addressed a poem striking the note of a new Puritan emigration:

> " We cross the prairie as of old
>   The pilgrims crossed the sea,
> To make the West, as they the East,
>   The homestead of the free!"

The issue was joined at last between the ideals of slavery and anti-slavery, and the conflict of *force,* not argument merely, was begun in blood, upon the soil of Kansas. It would be an error to regard this outcry in the North as an expression of anti-slavery sentiment merely. National patriotism created intense irritation at the breaking of a solemn agreement, and this was the dominant feeling. Yet it was the ideal of anti-slavery, nevertheless, whether openly acknowledged or not, that permitted and caused this popular expression.

In the next few years, the old Whig party, its ideals forgotten, was discredited, the new Republican party, vigorously acclaiming ideals, was born, and in this political disruption the Democratic party, largely controlled by Southern politicians, won the election of 1856. Then followed a rapid readjustment of party lines, and in 1860, the Republicans inheriting the force of the Free Soilers, and strengthened by defections from Whigs and Democrats, elected Lincoln, in spite of Southern threats of secession. The strength of this new party lay in the courage of its convictions and ideals, and its chief cry was "no slavery in the territories." Whatever may be said, however largely other elements may be magnified, however clearly evidence may show other motives determining Lincoln's vote, whatever quotation may be made from the press, the platform, and Lincoln's own words to prove that the election did not mean a desire for abolition in the old states,—yet the historical fact remains that it was the ideal of anti-slavery which had brought this upheaval in national politics.

In my previous lecture, I stated that the ideal of nationality in the Civil War rose above all other ideals, and fought and won that war. But this involves no denial of the power of the ideal of anti-slavery, nor of its victory in the election of 1860. The instinct and understanding of the South were correct. Whatever the immediate results, slavery must ultimately disappear *within this Union,* and the South, seeking to preserve its ideal of slavery, sought safety in the constitutional doctrines of state liberty, and the right of secession. And the South was wholly sincere, basing its defense of an institution it believed beneficent upon that same Declaration of Independence to which the anti-slavery leaders appealed. Jefferson Davis, in his farewell speech to the Senate, January 21, 1861, said, "The sacred Declaration of Independence has been invoked to maintain the position of the equality of the races." This interpretation of the word "equality" he repudiated, and in defense of the secession of his state, Mississippi, he asserted that she but acted under the sense of one of the very grievances that had caused the Revolution of 1776. In proof of this he cited, among the grievances against King George the Third, one in which he was accused of "endeavoring of late to stir insurrection among our slaves." Davis was in error in thinking there was such an item in the Declaration, for that to which he referred reads, "He has excited domestic insurrections amongst us," and in Jefferson's original draft this was "He has incited treasonable insurrections of our fellow citizens, with the allurements of forfeiture and confiscation of our property,"—clearly no reference to slaves, while in the very next section of Jefferson's draft, though omitted in the final form of the Declaration, is a vigorous attack upon King George III for maintaining the African slave trade against the protests of the colonies. Certainly Davis was no historical student, but the very boldness of his error reveals his sincerity, and the intensity of Southern conviction. He hoped for a peaceful secession, but if the North refused this, he affirmed of the South that "putting our trust in God, and in our own firm hearts and strong arms, we will vindicate the right as best we may."

"It is joyous in the midst of perilous times to look around upon a people united in heart, where one purpose of high resolve animates and actuates the whole, when the sacrifices to be made are not weighed in the balance, against honor, right, liberty, and equality. Obstacles may retard, but they can not long prevent, the progress of a movement sanctioned by its justice and sustained by a virtuous people. Reverently let us invoke the God of our fathers to guide and protect us in our efforts to perpetuate the principles which by His blessing they were able to vindicate, establish, and transmit to their posterity; and with a continuance of His favor, ever gratefully acknowledged, we may hopefully look forward to success, to peace, to prosperity."

In these inspiring words, Jefferson Davis concluded his inaugural address of February 18, 1861. He voiced the ideal of liberty. Alexander Stephens, as vice-president, upheld the ideal of slavery. Acknowledging that the fathers of the constitution might have had in mind the ultimate extinction of slavery, he said:

"Our new government is founded upon exactly the opposite idea; its foundations are laid, its corner-stone rests upon the great truth that the negro is not equal to the white man, that slavery—subordination to the superior race,—is his natural and normal condition.

"This, our new government, is the first in the history of the world based upon this great physical, philosophical, and moral truth. . . . Our Confederacy is founded upon principles in strict conformity with these views. This stone, which was rejected by the first builders, 'is become the chief of the corner,' the real 'corner-stone' in our new edifice."

Here was the expression of an ideal, largely created by the anti-slavery movement in the North. Who will say that the ideal of anti-slavery was not a powerful force in our history? Yet at this same moment the abolition leaders had hushed their voices. At first jubilant over the coming disruption of the Union, Wendell Phillips had said that the flag of the United States might now be placed as a curio in the museum of the Historical Society. But three months later, April 21, 1861, a convert to the higher ideal of nationality, in the same public hall, he renounced his stand, declaring "today the abolitionist is merged in the citizen." Later he acknowledged the ideal nature of the conflict on both sides.

"The War for the Union," he said, "was . . . inevitable; in one sense, nobody's fault; the inevitable result of past training, the conflict of ideas, millions of people grappling each other's throats, every soldier in each camp certain that he is fighting for an idea which holds the salvation of the world. . . ."

There is no need to dwell upon the later phases of the conflict between these opposing ideals. The Emancipation Proclamation was a war measure, but it became effective only as territory was conquered by the North. During the progress of the war, the North, self-righteous, became sentimental over the negro, and at its conclusion legislated for him on lines of sentiment, rather than of science. But error in the application of an ideal does not refute its actual historical force. Let us turn again to the statement that geography and industrialism created and determined this struggle.

The economic historian has said that, from 1840 to 1860, class interests ruled more than ever before in our history, and that "moral consciousness" was at its lowest ebb. For this astounding assertion, he should have piled proof on proof, for it is directly contrary to accepted history. Possibly he mistook the shattering of traditions, the unrest of the time, for decay, when it was, in fact, the first evidence of new life. As I read this period, it was one of intense, even fierce, spiritual expression, manifesting itself in the ideals of nationality, manifest destiny, democracy, anti-slavery, and in a wonderful home missionary movement. Economic interests can not, do not, explain the growth of anti-slavery sentiment after 1840. The deeper economic interest, the contest of free against slave labor, may, indeed, as Karl Marx perceived, have been an element in the struggle, but it was an element almost wholly without influence on men's minds, for it was unrecognized by the mass. The more immediate economic interest of the North, whether of the cotton lords of New England, or of the business world in general, was *against* the agitation of the slavery question, and it is the obvious economic interest, not the basic one, that makes itself felt in political action.

The real truth is that, until the thirties, New England religious dogmatism, and the controversies in regard to it, held intellectual interests, to the exclusion of humanitarian sentiment in regard to slavery. Meanwhile the economic interest of New England, centered in her manufactories, tended to a defense of slavery. Abolition and anti-slavery were nowhere more bitterly denounced. It is true, no doubt, that Southern industrial conditions, agitated by the anti-slavery outcry, deepened Southern conviction of the morality of slavery, but it is not true that the absence of those conditions in New England created an anti-slavery ideal. That ideal was, rather, an intellectual and spiritual conception,—the result of a thousand years, it may be, of the slow development of human thought, and of a thought always laboring under the necessity of differentiating good from evil. The ideals of personal liberty, and of humanity, were *not* created by the "boulder-strewn soil" of New England. They already existed there, and when directed to the question of slavery, won a victory in men's minds over the economic interest of the community.

III

MANIFEST DESTINY—AN EMOTION

MANIFEST DESTINY—AN EMOTION

Before attempting a narration of the origin and growth of the ideal of manifest destiny, in its territorial expansion aspect, I find it necessary, in order that its later phases may be understood, to state explicitly what I conceive to be the essence of the ideal of manifest destiny as a force in our history, actively recognized at the time it was exercised. The materialistic historians attribute the westward movement of population to a mere desire for the "gross comforts of material abundance." In answer to this, President Woodrow Wilson, the historian, has written:

"The obvious fact is that for the creation of the nation the conquest of her proper territory from Nature was first necessary; and this task, which is hardly yet completed, has been idealized in the popular mind. A bold race has derived inspiration from the size, the difficulty, the danger of the task."

In my opinion both of these interpretations are in error. The purely materialistic historian loses sight of the fact that the people who took part in the westward movement up to 1830, carried with them the ideal of democracy. Mr. Wilson, regarding this wonderful movement from the point of view of

later times, himself feeling the joy the pioneer must
have had in the mere subjection of the soil, admir-
ing his energy and courage, has depicted the movement in colors that serve to idealize it. But it is
an error to assert that our understanding, our idealization, of events and conditions was also the conscious understanding and idealization of the men
who were participants in those events and conditions. We of the present age rightly regard as
heroic the American migration from East to West,
and exalt the personal virtues of the men who
led,—and of the women, those "Mothers of a
Forest Land, whose bosoms pillowed *Men!*" But
an ideal, unless it is consciously held by the actors,
can not be considered as a living force on men's
minds in their political activities. Now I very
much doubt whether a man who "moved west,"
ever felt any "inspiration from the size, the difficulty, the danger of the task," and I certainly do
not believe that before 1830, in thus moving west,
he was at all consciously influenced by an ideal of
expanding national territory. The inspiration
which he did carry west with him was that of
democracy, and when by 1830 there had been
added the inspiration of nationality, the two oper-
ated to create a new element in manifest destiny,
and that new element was territorial expansion,—
a continent-wide national destiny. The westward
movement did not create this new ideal, it was but

the necessary preliminary condition in which certain
inspirations, already held, took on a new form.
It follows from this that I do not consider the
mere shifting of population a result of the ideal
of manifest destiny. That ideal included, up to
about 1830, the sense of democracy and a belief in
its superiority; afterwards, a desire to expand it,
and to increase national power by territorial
acquisition. The ideal of democracy and its manifestations, I reserve for a later lecture. The present
lecture is primarily concerned, then, with the emotion of territorial expansion,—the emotion of
manifest destiny. But it is to be understood that
in each step forward in our territorial growth since
1800, there was a general belief that democracy was
expanding as well as national boundaries.

*   *   *   *   *   *

The sense of destiny is an attribute of all nations
and all peoples. If we could penetrate beyond the
veil of recorded history, and grasp the emotions of
tribes and races, of whom it is known only that
they existed, probably we should find that these
tribes also felt themselves a people set apart for
some high purpose. Possibly even the cannibal,
as he sacrifices his victim, satisfies both his physical
and his spiritual being,—though it is unlikely that
the victim appreciates the service he is rendering.
Among civilized peoples, national destiny has fre-

quently been accompanied by cannibalistic rites,—
also with an equal ignorance of a service performed
by the absorbed. Certainly there is no great nation
today that has not a belief in its destiny, both in
respect to territory and of peculiar function. The
larger nations seek "a place in the sun" for their
peoples. The smaller are content to feel that their
existence, as now established, is a manifestation of
providence, and urge this against absorption
threatened by powerful neighbors. But all nations
that are worth anything, always have had, and
always will have, some ideal of national destiny,
and without it, would soon disappear, and would
deserve their fate.

America has felt herself destined for various
high purposes. In early colonial times, the New
England communities felt more than all else that
they were destined to occupy and preserve a small
section of the earth, where those of like religious
faith and practice could realize, without governmental interference, certain religious ideals. There
were few who thought of a separate national existence from England, and it was not until shortly
before the war of independence that there was any
general conception of governmental ideals different
from those of Great Britain. Even after independence was won, the eyes of America were still
unconsciously turned toward the old world, the
colonial instinct was still dominant, and it was only

after the war of 1812 that America turned her gaze inward upon herself. At once she felt and expressed her "peculiar destiny,"—at first as the chosen servant of the spreading ideal of democracy, later in terms of territorial greatness. Militant patriotism came to reinforce this sense of a special national function in the cause of civilization, and that patriotism pictured Great Britain as the hereditary foe of America. This was inevitable, since stories of valor or of suffering were necessarily connected with the only nation with whom we had fought. The schoolboy, in selected orations and poetry, was trained in this hostility towards England,—a hostility which was, in fact, merely one expression of nationality. Captain Hall, an Englishman traveling in the United States, in 1827, was both amused and astonished on visiting the Boston public schools, that a boy called up to "speak" for the visitor's pleasure, should recite a "furious philippic" against Great Britain, while a second youth gave an oration beginning:

"For eighteen hundred years the world had slumbered in ignorance of liberty, and of the true rights of freemen. At length America arose in all her glory, to give the world the long desired lesson!"

The intolerance of America in thus training its youth in fixed hostility to old England, the arrogance of the young nation, in a new land, assuming to instruct the old world, were truly amusing, yet back of all bombast and back of all crudity of expression was the sincere conviction that America was destined to be the greater nation, that it would accomplish greater things, that it could offer exceptional enlightenment and bestow unusual favors.

The period from 1830 to 1860 is usually regarded as that in which the ideal of manifest destiny most affected our history. During these years the term "manifest destiny" vaguely expressed the sense of the American people that their government gave an example to the world of the success of the democratic principle, and that power went hand in hand with democracy. Previous to 1830 the westward shifting of population did not imply a belief in a continent-wide country. Year after year American citizens laboriously surmounted the Appalachian range, sought the sources of the streams flowing to the west, and followed these to the land of promise. Until the completion of the Erie Canal the bulk of this movement was from the middle and southern states, a poor white population finding in the rich soil of Kentucky, or Indiana, or Ohio, an improved industrial opportunity, and founding settlements marked by extreme simplicity and equality. Gradually the wide domain of the territory east of the Mississippi was dotted with villages and farms, and by 1830 the frontier had moved across the river into the lands of the

Louisiana purchase.   After 1825, there came an increased northern migration, swelled by a steady stream of British immigrants, though this last was never large and almost ceased temporarily in 1830. The German immigration of the early thirties added to this wave of humanity moving westward.   But as yet there was room for all, and save for the uneasy frontiersman, restless if he had any neighbors, there could be no pressing need, for many years to come, of lands beyond the established boundaries of the country.

The controversy with Great Britain in the twenties over Oregon made clear that America, before 1830, had no thought of continental dominion and regarded as a dreamer the man who would still expand the national domain.   Benton, senator from Missouri, was such a dreamer, but dared not give expression to his dream.   In 1825, Russia, by treaties with England and the United States, had renounced her claims south of 54° 40′, leaving the two remaining powers in joint possession.   At once a bill was introduced in Congress for the military occupation of Oregon.   A few supported it, more were opposed, but the great majority were wholly indifferent.   Dickerson of New Jersey made the principal speech against the measure.   "We have not," he said, "adopted a system of colonization, and it is to be hoped we never shall.   Oregon can never be one of the United States.   If we extend

our laws to it, we must consider it as a colony. . . .
Is this territory of Oregon ever to become a state,
a member of this Union? Never. The Union is
already too extensive." He then entered upon a
calculation to prove the utter impossibility of a
representative in Congress for Oregon, since mere
distance would prove an effective barrier. Postu-
lating that a representative must visit his constit-
uents at least once a year, he stated the distance
from the mouth of the Columbia to Washington
as 4650 miles, or 9300 for the round trip. According to federal law granting mileage payment to
congressmen, the average rate of travel was then
twenty miles per day, but supposing the Oregonian
to exceed this rate of speed, and to maintain the
high average of thirty miles, "This," continued
Dickerson, "would allow the member a fortnight
to rest himself at Washington before he should
commence his journey home. . . . It would be more
expeditious, however, to come by water round Cape
Horn, or to pass through Behrings Straits, round
the North coast of this Continent to Baffin's Bay,
thence through Davis Straits to the Atlantic, and
so on to Washington. It is true, this passage is
not yet discovered, except upon our maps,—but it
will be as soon as Oregon shall be a State."

Benton himself was oppressed by the remote-
ness of the territory, and standing almost alone in
the Senate, did not dare to profess a belief that

Oregon could ever be admitted to the Union. He asserted, rather, that "the greatest of all advantages to be derived from the occupation of this country, is in the exclusion of foreign powers from it." He did assert, however, that Oregon would soon be settled, either by European or by American colonists, and declared that it lay with Congress to determine which. Seeking to persuade his hearers to action he pictured American settlement on lines of ultimate separation from the United States. The successive steps would be military occupation, settlements and a civil territorial government, then clamors against the hardship of dependence upon a government so remote as Washington, and finally independence willingly granted by the mother country. Continuing his plea for action, Benton even acknowledged that the Rocky Mountains formed the natural limit of the United States. To the west of that line, this offspring of our institutions would guard our interests, and America would have cause to rejoice in having aided "in the erection of a new Republic, composed of her children, speaking her language, inheriting her principles, devoted to liberty and equality, and ready to stand by her side against the combined powers of the old world."

The long journey to Oregon was indeed a barrier to settlement in the twenties. The next step of the American advance was to the southwest rather than

to the northwest, and marks the faint beginnings
of the expressed ideal of a territorial manifest destiny, later developed to great proportions. There
were several elements merged in the American
interest in, and desire for, Texas; the impulsion of
the westward movement as lands further west and
south became available to settlers; the natural and
hopeful interest of Southerners who urged and
anticipated annexation; and, in addition, the call
of manifest destiny,—the yearning for power and
territory. For a time, however, the more cautious
and conservative opinion of the older states checked
the cry for annexation and Texas was forced to rest
under a separate sovereignty. Meanwhile, as evidence that the earlier movement on Texas was no
mere slavery conspiracy, as Northern historians of
the time declared, but was a manifestation of
revived restlessness, and of a popular belief in the
destined further expansion of America, we have
but to note the conditions of the Canadian rebellion
of 1837.

The causes of this miniature revolution do not
call for narration, except to explain that in both
Lower and Upper Canada the leaders proclaimed
their admiration of American institutions and
claimed that they were fighting for self-government.
Easily defeated in Canada, they fled across the
border, appealing to the "sympathy and generosity
of a liberty-loving people," and there renewed their

efforts to overthrow the Canadian governments. The revolution began in the last months of 1837. At that time the United States was in the throes of the most serious financial crisis in her history; everywhere there were great numbers of idle men, and as filibusters and meddlesome fighters are always recruited from the idle and lawless classes, there were many sympathizers, with empty pockets, ready to join the adventure to "redeem Canada." Yet there were higher motives, and higher-minded men concerned in the movement. MacKenzie, the leader of the revolution in Upper Canada, was a man of unquestioned honor and high ideals, and won the sympathy of the American idealist who saw in his plans an effort to spread American political principles. In addition, there were those who thought that the revolution might be a first step toward the admission of Canada to the Union. The emotion of territorial greatness was beginning to be felt, and the riff-raff of the northern frontier, from Vermont to Michigan, were encouraged by the expression of ideals of democracy and expansion, in public meetings and in the press. The government at Washington condemned this border excitement, but at first was badly hampered in suppressing it, owing to antiquated and ineffective neutrality laws.

"The American," says Mr. Bryce, "likes excitement for its own sake and goes wherever he can

find it." Americans of this spirit were the first to
hasten to the call of the Canadian revolutionists,
but their number was soon increased by the unem-
ployed, and even by some who saw in the event a
chance to attack privilege and property,—as the
barber of Plattsburg, moulding musket balls, and
rejoicing that "one ball would do the business of
a man worth £2000 a year." The first rendezvous
of these would-be American-Canadian "Patriots"
was Navy Island, just above Niagara Falls on the
Canadian side of the river. Here a camp of the
"grand army of invasion" was established, and here
a steamboat, the *Caroline,* carried supplies and men
from the American side. In order to cut off this
communication, a small Canadian force crossed the
river in the night to the spot where the *Caroline*
was anchored, cut her out, towed her into mid-
stream, set her on fire, and left her to drift over
the falls. The affair created a terrific excitement.
American territory had been invaded, her sacred
soil polluted by the myrmidons of a despotic government. The Rochester *Democrat,* inspired to
poetic frenzy, wrote:

> " As over the shelving rocks she broke,
>   And plunged in her turbulent grave,
> The slumbering genius of Freedom woke,
>   Baptized in Niagara's wave,
> And sounded her warning tocsin far,
> From Atlantic's shore to the polar star."

For genius immersed in Niagara's wave, this was indeed a far cry. But the "Caroline Affair" was in truth a serious one, since it called for revenge, thus adding strength to the "patriot" cause.

On the Canadian side, the cry arose that Great Britain must gird herself to defend monarchical institutions and territory. Lieutenant-Governor Head, of Upper Canada, was as rabid and as melodramatic as the editor of the *Democrat*. He pictured this petty conflict as a contest between republican and monarchical institutions. In a public address he asserted:

"The People of Upper Canada detest Democracy. . . . They are perfectly aware that there exist in the Lower Province one or two individuals who inculcate the Idea that *this* Province is about to be disturbed by the Interference of Foreigners [Americans], whose Power and whose Numbers will prove invincible.

"In the name of every Regiment of militia in Upper Canada I publicly promulgate—Let them come if they dare."

"The enemy of the British Constitution," he said, "is its low-bred Antagonist, Democracy in America."

Later, in reporting a skirmish between a few Canadians and revolutionists, part of whom were American recruits, he wrote:

"The Republicans stood their ground until the monarchical troops arrived within about twenty yards of them, when, abandoning their position, as also their Principle that all men are born equal, they decamped in the greatest confusion."

As apparently there were no shots exchanged in this fearful battle, the case does indeed seem one of those rare instances where principles were the sole contenders. Surely, if the American was fond of "twisting the Lion's tail," Head had revenge in "plucking the Eagle's feathers."

From a perspective of seventy-five years, the American relation to the Canadian rebellion seems ephemeral,—serio-comic. Yet the disturbances along the border gave evidence of a real intensity of feeling, and a genuine passion for expansion. The trouble lasted for two years, and was contemporary with a renewed dispute over the Maine boundary. There now came to the surface the feeling, later very powerful, that American destiny ran counter to that of England on this continent, and that one or the other must give way. Cushing, speaking in Congress in 1839, asserted that England was pursuing a definite policy of irritation, wherever she could press in upon the United States,— over the Maine boundary, in the Northwest, where the Indians were causing trouble, and in Oregon.

"Unless," he said, "this all grasping spirit of universal encroachment on the part of Great

Britain be arrested, either by moderation in her councils, or by fear, the time must and will come, when her power and ours cannot co-exist on the continent of North America."

This meant that the United States would be forced to expand in defense of what she already possessed,—but back of this lay the desire of expansion for its own sake. In the late thirties this demand for territory and power was nation-wide, and though it was but one of the causes of the border troubles of that time, it first found expression in them. Failing to achieve results in Canada, interest easily turned to the southern border, where Texas waited.

When, in 1836, Texas declared her independence from Mexico, the Americans who had established that independence, strongly desired annexation. The offer was declined, but the migration into this new country rapidly increased, and the newcomers reinforced annexation sentiment both in Texas and in the United States. By 1842, Texas had secured recognition from the stronger powers as an independent state, and to two of these powers, England and the United States, the future of Texas became a matter of great importance. Slavery existed, and cotton seemed destined to be the chief industrial product. England, hoping to free herself from dependence on American cotton, and at the same time establish a barrier to further American expansion, naturally encouraged Texan independence. The United States, while rejoicing over this new Anglo-Saxon nation, was yet in a doubtful position in regard to it.   Mexico stubbornly refused to acknowledge Texan independence, and annexation might involve us in a war.   Northern feeling was against a new slave state, so large that several slave states seemed then inevitable.   In the South there rapidly developed enthusiasm for annexation on the score of Southern political influence, and the sentiment of manifest destiny was appealed to,—an effective appeal, since the hearts of all our Western people beat responsive to the cry.   By 1842, the South was determined to have Texas, and the "Texan game," as Northern opponents termed it, was begun.

Manifest destiny was a strong factor in annexation sentiment, but a more specific argument was found in the national jealousy of England.   Tyler and Calhoun raised the cry of British opposition, with more justice than the partisans of anti-slavery admitted.   Great Britain did indeed hope that in Texas she would find a block to the increasing power of America, and even dreamed of inducing Texas to abolish slavery.   Elliot, the British diplomat in Texas, confined his official efforts, however, to a preservation of the independence of Texas.   He sought to check annexation sentiment, picturing the future greatness of an independent

Texas. British colonists were introduced, but they were few in number compared with the steady stream from the United States, and, as Elliot himself sorrowfully confessed, they were wholly inferior in the art of pioneering. Like Peter Simple, the British colonist "preferred to walk, rather than to run, toward his goal, for fear he would arrive out of breath." Elliot, marveling at the difficulties and crudities of the American push westward, said "they jolt and jar terrifically in their progress, but *on they do get*." With the coming of new American settlers, it became certain that Texas herself cared more for annexation than for independence. In the United States the sentiment of expansion grew steadily in strength, and though Calhoun, raising the cry of British interference, was at first defeated by the conservative and anti-slavery elements in the Senate, the campaign of Polk in 1844, when the rivalry with England for Oregon was also played upon, settled the destiny of Texas. In that campaign was heard, at last, no mere feeble and isolated assertion of a continent-wide destiny, but a positive and general profession of faith in the inevitable progress of democratic institutions and "Anglo-Saxon" ideals, destined to triumph over monarchical principles and inferior races. The clap-trap political oratory of this campaign is distressing to the patriotic historian, and I refrain from quotation, but it must be recognized that such oratory was used and was effective, simply because it reflected an American emotion. Manifest destiny, in terms of expansion, suddenly revealed itself as a powerful sentiment, against which the conservative minority struggled in vain. Nor was the expression of this sentiment confined to the political orator. Lyman Beecher, in a sermon enumerating the vices threatening American life, yet claimed for America a superior position among nations. "Our very beginning," he said, "was civilized, learned and pious." And even yet America is

". . . still the richest inheritance which the mercy of God continues to the troubled earth. Nowhere beside, if you search the world over, will you find so much real liberty; so much equality; so much personal safety, and temporal prosperity; so general an extension of useful knowledge; so much religious instruction; so much moral restraint; and so much divine mercy, to make these blessings the power of God, and the wisdom of God unto salvation."

If these blessings were indeed peculiar to America, what reasonable opposition could exist to carrying them into new territory?

Polk's election determined the future of Texas, and Great Britain regretfully relinquished her hope of a barrier state, yet consoled herself with the thought that mere territorial weight would break

the Union in fragments. But with Oregon it was
a different matter. During the campaign, Democratic orators had declared for the extreme American claim,—"fifty-four forty or fight," and to this
England would by no means agree. Southern
leaders, gratified as to Texas, now sought to quiet
the expansion sentiment they had used with so
much success. Previously, in 1843, a bill for the
organization of Oregon, offering lands to settlers,
had been introduced in Congress. Senator McDuffie
of South Carolina, who saw in slavery the "bulwark
of republican institutions," was against it, saying:

"I would not give a pinch of snuff for the whole
territory. I wish to God we did not own it, I wish
it was an impassable barrier to secure us against
the intrusion of others. . . . Do you think your
honest farmers in Pennsylvania, New York, or even
Ohio or Missouri, will abandon their farms to go
upon any such enterprise as that?   God forbid!"

At the time McDuffie made this speech, other
Southerners were more reserved, but no sooner had
Tyler despatched the offer to receive Texas into
the Union than the sentiments of McDuffie were
revived.   But Polk, a determined expansionist,
already planning to go far beyond Texas, and to
carry American territory to the Pacific in the South
as well as in the North, stood firmly for Oregon.
Apparently he intended to exact the extreme
American claim, and hostilities with England

seemed near. At the same time, Mexico, still claiming Texas as her own, threatened war, while Texas unexpectedly delayed a formal acceptance of the annexation proposal. The situation seemed dangerous, and with a prospect of war on both northern and southern borders, wisdom urged caution. Horace Greeley, opposed to slavery expansion, argued in the *New York Tribune* against any expansion, citing Benton's speech of 1825 to prove that the Rocky Mountains formed a natural boundary. Winthrop, in Congress, answered the expansionist dogma, "The finger of God never points in a direction contrary to the extension of the glory of the Republic," by quoting:

> " Glory is like a circle in the water,
>   Which never ceaseth to enlarge itself,
>   Till by broad spreading it disperse to naught."

But Greeley and Winthrop were upheld by the anti-slavery faction alone. The *New York Sun* and the *New York Herald* strongly approved annexation and expansion, the latter asserting, "Our march is *onward* for centuries to come, *still onward*—and they who do not keep up with us, must fall behind and be forgotten,"—apparently a reference to Mexico. According to the *Evening Post,* Greeley stood alone in the North: "With the exception of the *Tribune* . . . there is not a press in the Union which does not say Oregon is ours

and must be maintained." Polk had no intention
of drifting into war with England, and, after a due
amount of bluster, agreed to the forty-ninth parallel
as the proper boundary of Oregon; but before this
was known, the *Herald,* with an eye on all North
America, expressed the hope that war would ensue
with both England and Mexico.

"The destiny of the Republic," it stated, "is
apparent to every eye. Texas Annexation must be
consummated, and the immediate results of that
event may only precipitate the subjugation of the
whole continent, despite of all the opposing efforts
of the despotic dynasties of Europe."

Thus we were "destined" to have Mexico and
Canada sometime;—why not now? The *Washington Union,* the administration paper, while
relations with England and Mexico were still unde-
termined, expressed deep suspicion of Great
Britain, and asserted that no nation could thwart
American "destiny."

"The march of the Anglo-Saxon race is onward.
They must in the event, accomplish their destiny,—
spreading far and wide the great principles of self-
government, and who shall say how far they will
prosecute the work?"

Mingled with this emotion of destiny there was
evident the appeal which the "West" made as a

land of opportunity. A bit of verse appearing in a St. Louis paper was widely reprinted in the East:

"COME OUT TO THE WEST."

" Come forth from your cities, come out to the West;
  Ye have hearts, ye have hands—leave to Nature the rest.
  The prairie, the forest, the stream at command—
  'The world is too crowded!'—pshaw! come and *take*
    land.

" Come travel the mountain, and paddle the stream;
  The cabin shall smile, and the corn-patch shall gleam;
  'A wife and six children?'—'tis wealth in your hand!
  Your ox and your rifle—out West and take land!"

Possibly it was by such means that Martin Chuzzlewit was induced to buy a corner lot in "Eden." The West had cast a glamor over the eyes of the nation, and the greater the distance, the more alluring the prospect. But with Oregon secured, and with Texas and California made definitely ours in the progress of the war with Mexico, Polk was satisfied and hastened the peace negotiations, that the fever of expansion should not rise too high. The Southern leaders were accustomed to bewail the fact that they would always be damned in history, since the historical writing was all done in New England. The South has indeed been thus damned for the annexation of Texas and the Mexican War, but in the former case alone can the slavery interest be regarded as an important factor.

Manifest destiny was the one great leading force in the war with Mexico.

At the end of the war, except for the extreme anti-slavery faction, there was united glorification in the power, and in the territorial greatness of America. The emotion of manifest destiny was at its height. Foreign observers were astounded by the national self-confidence, and appalled by the actual power of the United States. Warburton, an English traveler, arriving in America "in ignorance," as he himself says, went away astonished and fearful.

"We cannot," he writes, "conceal from ourselves that in many of the most important points of national capabilities they beat us; they are more energetic, more enterprising, less embarrassed with class interests, less burthened by the legacy of debt. This country, as a field for increase of power, is in every respect so infinitely beyond ours that comparison would be absurd." . . . All things "combine to promise them, a few years hence, a degree of strength which may endanger the existing state of things in the world. They only wait for matured power, to apply the incendiary torch of Republicanism to the nations of Europe."

Warburton overstates American desire to meddle in European affairs, yet he expresses American belief in the contagious qualities of the ideal of self-government. Witness our enthusiasm over the European revolutions of 1848, when press, pulpit, and Congress gave credit to American ideals and institutions,—being woefully ignorant of the many sources of the most confused revolutionary movement in history. Yet there is a touch of truth in the theory that the prosperity and power of America, looked upon as a test of the success of her democratic institutions, were an influence in expanding liberalism in Europe. Perhaps this was our most grandiloquent period. Here was this vast country,—its riches untold, seaports on two oceans, the one ideal form of government, and possibilities of power beyond telling. After the absorption of so much territory in so short a time, America summed up her material blessings and was satisfied. But she hoped for dominion even beyond material things. A handful of people as compared with the great powers of Europe, she arrogated to herself leadership in the world of ideas, and proposed to make herself respected and feared in the family of Nations. Clay best expressed it in 1850, saying:

"Our country has grown to a magnitude, to a power and greatness, such as to command the respect, if it does not awe the apprehensions of the powers of the earth, with whom we come in contact."

The ebb of the tide of expansion craze began with the acquisition of the Pacific Coast. The discovery of gold in California drew in a new direction the bulk of that adventurous population which had heretofore worried our neighbors. Before that discovery, Polk, in 1847, had advocated a waterway across the Isthmus of Panama, and Francis Lieber urged America not to be afraid of her future, and to build the canal, writing:

> "Let the vastness not appal us;
> Greatness is thy destiny.
> Let the doubters not recall us:
> Venture suits the free."

The gold rush at once forced into prominence the question of transit by the Isthmus, and the Clayton-Bulwer treaty was signed with England, looking toward a canal. A ten-years' dispute as to the interpretation of that treaty followed, and Central America became the scene of a new "American movement," with William Walker, the "grey-eyed man of destiny," as the leading actor in filibustering expeditions, having for their object a tropical expansion, and finding favor in the South. Cuba also was an objective, but all this aftermath of the expansion craze was checked by the political exigencies of the dangerous situation within the United States, when the Kansas-Nebraska controversy arose.

Meanwhile Americans, generally, were proudly conscious of power, and of territorial greatness, and were not unduly modest in expressing this consciousness. Manifest destiny has indeed a characteristic of American humor,—exaggeration. The Englishman defined American humor as "merely a big lie,"—but he missed the fact that, to the American, the "big lie" was never quite an absolute impossibility. It was thus with the expression of the ideal of manifest destiny,—the bombast, however apparently absurd, was never wholly insincere, though it was tinctured with the love of humorous exaggeration for its own sake. This puzzled the English observer and he sometimes took American talk at its face value, as when the House of Lords solemnly recorded its indignation at an American proposal to repudiate all debts to foreign nations, on the ground that such creditors were fully recompensed in having aided in the spread of American civilization. The editorial in a Dubuque, Iowa, paper that inspired this British protest was a mere blatant absurdity and the editor must have been gratified, if he knew of it, to find his effort perpetuated in the pages of Hansard's Parliamentary Debates. Charles Dickens, in "Martin Chuzzlewit," revelled in the opportunity to caricature our assumption of superiority, and of the all-pervading influence of our institutions. Martin, under the guidance of Colonel Diver, editor of the *New York Rowdy Journal,* has made the acquaintance of several of "the most remarkable men of the country, sir," and has been astounded by their youth. At the dinner table in the boarding house, he is equally astounded to learn that the "little girl, like a doll," seated opposite, is the mother of two children. He expresses his wonder to Colonel Diver, who replies, "Yes, Sir, but some institutions develop human nature; others re-tard it." More serious English writers, accepting American estimate of the power and future expansion of the United States, struck the note of "hands across the sea," and declared a common destiny for the two nations, each in its own field. Charles Mackay, the "Ayrshire Poet," read at a banquet in Washington a poem called "John and Jonathan," disclaiming for John any wish to interfere with Jonathan's destiny:

" Take you the West and I the East,
    We'll spread ourselves abroad,
  With Trade and Spade, and wholesome laws,
    And faith in Man and God.

" Take you the West and I the East,
    We speak the self-same tongue
  That Milton wrote and Chatham spoke,
    And Burns and Shakespeare sung;
  And from our tongue, our hand, our heart,
    Shall countless blessings flow
  To light two darkened hemispheres
    That know not where they go."

The Civil War put a sudden end to the clamor for territorial expansion. The purchase of Alaska, in 1867, awoke no enthusiasm in American hearts.

It was generally spoken of as "Seward's Folly," and regarded as a recompense to Russia for her friendly attitude during the war. For thirty years America was occupied with industrial development, satisfied to retain for herself the blessing of her institutions, with no inclination to confer them by force on other nations. Then came the Spanish-American war. Whatever its origin, the war awoke again, but only for the moment, the emotion of manifest destiny. President McKinley, in a message to Congress, following the cession of the Philippines by Spain, expressed the national sentiment:

"The war," he said, "has brought us new duties and responsibilities which we must meet and discharge as becomes a great nation on whose growth and career from the beginning the Ruler of Nations has plainly written the high command and pledge of civilization. Incidental to our tenure in the Philippines is the commercial opportunity to which American statesmanship cannot be indifferent."

A shrill voice from the East protested, but these words express briefly the true inwardness of manifest destiny at all times in our history. Even more briefly put they might be condensed to, "God directs us,—perhaps it will pay."

*   *   *   *   *   *

If, in this lecture, I have seemed to present to you an ideal simply as a target for caricature and ridicule, I shall be unfair to my own conception of manifest destiny and its influence. It is true that, as an ideal embracing territorial expansion, I have little respect for it, though I do not agree with Lowell:

> " Thet all this big talk of our destinies
>   Is half on it ign'ance and t'other half rum,"

for it can not be denied that always there was present a spiritual exaltation, and not only the assertion, but the conviction of the superiority of American institutions.   But the taint of sordid motives was there too.   There was a golden ideal in the emotion, but there was also an alloy of baser metals. This criticism should not, however, lessen emphasis upon the force of the ideal of manifest destiny in American history, for whatever its origin, or however used, the ideal existed of and by itself.   No economic basis whatever can be found for it after the annexation of Texas, and even in that instance, the emotion played as great a part as industrial interests.   It was a fever in the blood that steadily rose, and was allayed only by the letting of blood.

In the introduction to this lecture I asserted that the westward movement, in and of itself, held no conscious ideal of a continent-wide destiny. Setting aside such a claim for that movement, there were, then, two phases of manifest destiny,—the earlier expressing merely the conviction of superiority in our form of government, and the greater happiness of our people; while the later phase carried with this belief the desire for new territory, and the responsibility of imposing upon other nations the benefits of our own. Present-day judgment repudiates the latter view, while holding firmly to the faith in our institutions, and to confidence in our future. In that ideal of manifest destiny,—a belief in our institutions, as the best in the world adapted to secure to *our* people "life, liberty, and the pursuit of happiness,"—we may still assert our faith. But in relation to those nations whose boundaries touch our own, or in whose peace and prosperity we have an interest, let us agree with Joseph Gilder's vision of the duty of America:

> "Be thou the guardian of the weak,
>   Of the unfriended, thou the friend;
>   No guerdon for thy valor seek,
>   No end beyond the avowèd end
>   Wouldst thou thy godlike power preserve,
>   Be godlike in the will to serve." *

* From *Harper's Weekly*. Copyright, 1900, by Harper & Brothers.

IV

RELIGION—A SERVICE

RELIGION—A SERVICE

Unlike other ideals, religious conviction in the nineteenth century has not found expression in any one distinct movement, nor in any one period. It is rather a diffused force working in and through all other forces,—and thus difficult to isolate. Naturally and necessarily, I turn to church movements, and to the activities of the clergy, for illustration, yet it is the custom and conduct of the people, rather than the leadership of the pulpit, that is vital.

In early colonial times church and state were so interwoven that religious expression and creeds were an essential part of citizenship. But with the spread of the principle of freedom of conscience, taking form in the separation of church and state, religion came to be regarded as something apart from the political life of the nation, and the pulpit as largely restricted from leadership in political action. This was an inevitable swing back of the pendulum from the point of clerical domination. The pulpit emphasized creed and dogma, devoting its mental energy to these topics, and paying little attention to acute questions of the day. The force of the clergy, in the affairs of state, disappeared, while to every church member the essential thing became the personal satisfaction derived from an accepted relation with God, looking toward happiness and perfection in a future life. This is not to say that conduct and character were neglected, nor that the broad term morality was divorced from civic duties. On the contrary, every religious-minded man sought to support his civic action by a reference to moral principles. Washington, in his farewell address, said, "I hold the maxim no less applicable to public than to private affairs, that honesty is always the best policy," and again, he stated, "Virtue or morality is a necessary spring of popular government." But Washington would have been the last to acknowledge religious dogma as a complete guide to civic duty. The reaction from religious despotism was excessive. Washington Irving, writing of the Puritan treatment of the Indians, has said, "They [the Indians] were sober, frugal, continent, and faithful to their word, but though they acted right habitually, it was all in vain unless they acted so by precept." The power of precept was still predominant in religion, but by the eighteenth century it had come to be limited to a profession of faith, and an observance of customary religious exercises. Neither pulpit nor people sought anxiously any longer for the expression of their religious convictions in civic life. To nations where church and state still held a relation which America had discarded, the decay of practical morality in America seemed inevitable. Such nations observed with scorn what seemed to them an irreconcilable contradiction between the keen business instincts of the Yankee, and his professions of religion. One of the oldest British jibes at America pictures the Yankee storekeeper as instructing his clerk, preparing for the business of the morrow, to "sand the sugar, flour the ginger, lard the butter, and then come in to prayers."

In summarizing American religion in the eighteenth century, the church historian, Prof. Williston Walker, asserts that century to have been more barren than any other in our history, stating that the older devotion and the "sense of a national mission" were gone, and that everywhere, while religious services were still largely attended, this attendance was due to habit and to respect for external formality. This being true, the natural prelude to a revival of the *force* of religion in national life was a revolt from the despotism of dogma, and from the dwarfing influence of unchanging creeds. The period was one of idealism for individual liberty stated in terms of Jeffersonian democracy. More than a century and a half earlier the argument of Thomas Hooker for a democratic form of government in both church and state, was "embodied in January, 1639, in the fundamental laws or first constitution of Connecticut."

"The foundation of authority is laid in the free consent of the people. The choice of the people's magistrates belongs to the people of God's own allowance. They who have the power to appoint magistrates have also the right to place bonds and limitations on the power and place unto which they call them."

This was no declaration of individual liberty within the church, but, by 1800, the democracy of church organization—independence of the authority of a church hierarchy—had paved the way for liberty of conscience. This latter ideal was closely related, intellectually, to the ideals of Jeffersonian democracy.

The most definite form in which individual religious liberty now expressed itself was Unitarianism, with Channing as its prophet. Dr. Samuel Eliot has recently defined the fundamental principle of Unitarianism as "freedom as the way, and character as the test of religion." This, in substance, was the essence of Jeffersonian democracy, also. In examining the origins of both Unitarianism and democracy, one is struck by the similarity of the terms employed, as, for example, the "sovereign citizen" and the "sovereign soul." A basic principle in both movements was a belief in the natural instinct of man toward good, rather than evil. Thus the protest of Unitarianism against the doctrine of natural depravity, taken in connection with the assertion of individual liberty, made the Unitarian movement seem a part,—even a manifestation, of the nation-wide tendency in political thought. To foreign observers, especially those from England, seeking causes and foretelling results, it seemed a foregone conclusion that Unitarianism was to be the religion of America.

Thomas Jefferson himself identified liberty in political and in religious faith. "Priests," using the term in the sense of a clergy claiming authority to determine creeds, Jefferson classified with "despots." "Sweep away," he wrote, "their gossamer fabrics of factitious religion, and they [priests] would catch no more flies," and he fully believed in the future of Unitarianism. Thus he said:

"The pure and simple unity of the creator of the universe, is now all but ascendant in the Eastern States; it is dawning in the West, and advancing toward the South; and I confidently expect that the present generation will see Unitarianism become the general religion of the United States." Again, he said: "I trust there is not a young man now living in the United States who will not die an Unitarian."

I have no intention of dilating upon religious controversies, nor of examining in detail the actual extent and influence of the Unitarian faith *per se*. We are all aware that Unitarian church organization did not spread as Jefferson prophesied, and indeed, that such organization was largely limited to a small section of New England. There are those who claim that the Unitarian tenet, "liberty," is today a characteristic of all Protestant churches, and that in this respect Unitarian faith has become a national faith. They assert that Bushnell contributed to Congregationalism that individual liberty which Channing had proclaimed. But with this question I have no concern. All that I would here indicate is that the sense of "liberty"—of breaking away from old traditions—was expressed at once, both in religion and in political theory. Nor were the religious leaders unconscious of this. Channing expressed it for himself in a line, when in 1830, distressed by the indifference of the young men of Harvard to the French revolution of that year, he recalled his own emotions in the earlier French revolution, and exclaimed that he was "always young for liberty."

Just as liberty in religion was contemporary with the ideal of liberty through democracy, so the wonderful outburst of national church organizations, and of humanitarian societies, was contemporary with the outburst of the ideal of nationality. It has been stated in a previous lecture that the ideal of nationality flowered in 1815, thereafter steadily developing. Before 1815 there had been sporadic missionary and humanitarian effort by isolated churches, but only one effort on a large

scale and that wholly altruistic rather than national.
This was the American Board of Foreign Missions
founded in 1810. But with the new sense of
nationality came the vision of national religious
effort. In 1816 the American Bible Society, previously a local organization, was expanded into a
national society. In 1824 came the Sunday School
Union; in 1825 the American Tract Society; 1826
saw the organization of the Home Missionary
Society, and of the American Temperance Society.
In 1828 an American Peace Society brought
together in one national organization various local
societies, among which was that of New York
founded in 1815 by David Low Dodge. By 1830
this national religious movement was in full swing,
though later years were to witness a marvelous
expansion.

Here, then, as in the case of Unitarianism, religious expression coincided in its ideals with other
national ideals. Yet judged by the sermons of the
clergy, religion in America, while democratic in
organization, while sharing in the ideal of personal
liberty, and while participating in the ideal of
nationality, was still largely dominated by the theory
that it was something distinct and apart from
active life,—a theory, in short, which emphasized
a future life at the expense of the present. The
pulpit still dwelt, to the exclusion of applied religion, upon the personal relation with God, with

personal salvation as its object. I do not wish to overemphasize this, but such study as I have been able to give to the period from 1830 to 1850 has convinced me that formal religion did not then lead in the world of ideals, nor even in the true moral purpose of a people eagerly seeking spiritual growth.

This conservatism of the pulpit might be illustrated by quotations from many sermons in which it was sought to combat all tendencies to the new either in theology or in religious expression, while the real business of the churches was asserted to be strictly limited to keeping alive man's consciousness of his spiritual relation to God. I do not suppose that today the parents of the young man about to enter college give him as a parting present Todd's "Students Manual,"—a very wise, and a very practical guide to conduct,—but in the period of which I write, and long after, it was a frequent gift. Now the Rev. John Todd was a noted clergyman, and one might expect after reading his "Students Manual" that he, at least, would have appreciated the opportunity offered to the pulpit for leadership in those new manifestations of moral consciousness animating the nation. Yet in 1833 he preached a sermon, entitled "The Pulpit.—Its Influence upon Society," which so clearly epitomizes the attitude of the bulk of the Protestant clergy that I cannot refrain from citing at least the heads of his discourse. The central thread of the sermon is that the chief service of the pulpit is confined to teaching man's relation to God, personal piety, and the hope of a future life, but in expanding this thought the preacher stated the function of the pulpit in specific fields: Firstly, the pulpit acts as the preserver of the Christian Sabbath, and inculcates a knowledge of the Scriptures. Secondly, the pulpit emphasizes the personal relation between God and man, and especially tends to convince man that God's eye is constantly upon him, judging his actions. Thirdly, the pulpit provides the best type of education for the youth of the land. Here the preacher referred to that education pursued in the pastor's study by boys preparing for college, and he strongly opposed the system of high schools then springing up in New England, stating that the proposed specialization of a teaching profession "would have one capital deficiency. They [the teachers] would understand human nature only as seen in the language and the history of the dead, and as seen in books." Fourthly, the pulpit preserves and makes proper use of the art of eloquence. Fifthly, the pulpit more than any other institution performs the service of "calling man into social, national, and religious existence." I would that the preacher had expanded his fifthly into many sermons, but he was content with a generalization in the briefest of all his "heads," and in conclusion

he reiterated the prevailing thought throughout,—
the duty of the pulpit to interpret and perpetuate
religious faith expressed in creed, that church
members, obedient in conduct to such creed, might
share in a future life of holiness and bliss. His
concluding words, apostrophizing the service of the
pulpit and the church, were:

"Here may our children and our children's children, to the latest posterity, come and be taught the
way of eternal life. . . . When our heads are pillowed in the grave, and others have followed us
here and filled these seats and retired, when these
walls shall have crumbled to the dust, . . . may
they, and we, all meet to rejoice together forever
and forever."

We also believe that religion necessarily must
emphasize future life, and that the source of all
moral motive, all high ideals, all humanitarian
effort, all progress, rests in such a belief. All that
I would here indicate is that one's personal salvation, to be secured by an acceptance of a faith, was
still emphasized in this period, to the sacrifice of
religious service in this life. The egotism of
religious conviction still overshadowed its altruism.

If we examine the columns of the newspapers
from 1830 to 1840, we will find a curious evidence,
in the advertisements of books on religion, of the
persistence of the extreme Puritan attitude and

language.   In the *National Intelligencer* for July
10, 1828, there appears the following:

"JAMES'S ANXIOUS ENQUIRER"

"The anxious Enquirer after Salvation.   Directed
and Encouraged, by John Angell James, new
edition.   Price 50 cents."

The same thought, and the same relation of church
member and pastor, is indicated in this advertise-
ment as in the sermon of the Rev. John Todd.
Soon, however, the ideal of democracy would forbid to the clergy such superior authority.   Oliver
Wendell Holmes, though with a different meaning,
puts in a nut-shell the equality of priest and layman,
when, describing the visit of the divinity student
to the sick chamber of the cripple, he wrote:

" 'Shall I pray with you?' said the student; a
little before he would have said, 'Shall I pray for
you?' "

The relation of the ideals of democracy and of
religious expression has frequently been commented
upon by historians, when comparing the appearance
of Jacksonian, as distinguished from Jeffersonian,
democracy, with the rapid growth in the West of
the Methodist and Baptist denominations, for the
members of these churches were drawn to them,

in part, by a common equality of industrial and intellectual simplicity. But more important than this, in an analysis of the force of the ideal of religion, is the renewal of contact between religious observance and everyday life. It was in the West, and in all denominations, that the churches began to resume a spiritual leadership in the intimate affairs of the nation. An English Congregational clergyman, visiting America in 1833, was startled in Cincinnati on witnessing a Fourth of July celebration in which the trade organizations of the city marched with banners and cheering to the church, under Lyman Beecher's pastorate, listened to a brief patriotic sermon and then entered on the customary celebration of Independence Day. He described the scene as an "extraordinary mixture of the secular and the spiritual; and it was a question whether the tendency was not to make religion worldly, rather than the worldly religious." But on reflection he concluded that the Western preacher was in the right, stating "Our true wisdom, in consulting the good of the people, lies, not in excluding their secular concerns and pleasures from religion, but in diffusing religion through the whole of them."

In the West there was indeed a greater intimacy between pulpit and people, a closer contact between church and civic society than existed in the East. In the West there had now developed, also, a religious movement intimately related to, and vitally affecting, national ideals. Initiated when the ideal of nationality began to grip American sentiment, Home Missions passed through a period of slow development until, about 1840, the opening of new and easier routes had brought a rapid increase of Western population. The Eastern churches, especially those of New England, responded to the call of Home Missions for aid in carrying the religious ideals of the East to this new Western land. The burden of that call was that the West must be made one with the East in religious faith and life, thus emphasizing still the primary object of preserving the ancient doctrines of the churches. But in the hearts of young men this call was effective, and consciously so, because of an enthusiasm for the ideal of nationality, while, though unconsciously at first, the ideal of active service in everyday living was forced upon the Home Missionary preacher, by the very conditions of his participation in the westward movement. If I were here to follow the method previously used in these lectures, and seek illustrations in the history of Yale College, and its inspirations, there would be no lack of great names and great enterprises to record. Yale was one of the two main sources of this religious crusade. But, born and educated in a state where I have not merely read, but know, the characteristics and influence of Home Missions, I turn for illustration to that other main spring of Home Missionary effort, Andover Theological Seminary, and to that group of young ministers leaving its halls, the Iowa Band, whose history, as has been well said, portrays "the romance of home missions." Let me tell, very briefly, what the Iowa Band was and what it did.

At Andover, in the spring of 1843, three young theological students were attracted by the idea of working together and in some new field. Looking over the ground they hit upon Iowa as practically virgin soil, and as graduation approached, their number had increased to eleven, animated by the inspiration of united religious service. On October 4, 1843, ten of them began the journey west, traveling by rail to Buffalo, thence by the lakes to Chicago, and then in wagons to the Mississippi, which they crossed in a canoe on October 23,—a total journey of nineteen days. From the six missionaries already in Iowa, they received a hearty welcome. Iowa was then a territory, the first white settlement dating but ten years earlier, in 1833. The only portion of the territory open to settlement was a strip about forty miles wide and two hundred miles long, bordering on the Mississippi. The population in 1840 was 42,500, of whom not over 2,000 were professing Christians. Here the Iowa Band was to labor, and it is of interest to note that, undecided when leaving Andover as to church organization, they almost immediately determined upon the Congregational form, as best adapted to the democratic instincts of a frontier community. It was not an easy task these young ministers, reared in cultured Eastern families, and trained in Eastern college halls, found facing them. A complete and rapid readjustment of the whole ministerial point of view was necessary. One of them had thought out his plan of living in advance. "I am going to Iowa," he said, "and, when I get there, I am going to have my study and library. Then I am going to write two sermons a week; and, when the Sabbath comes, I am going to preach them, and the people, if they want the gospel, must come to hear." His first home was in a Christian household where there was but one living room, in a corner of which, partitioned by a quilt, he found his study and bedroom; and his study chair was a saddle, for he had to seek his hearers, not they him. Travel was on foot or horseback, by Indian trails or blazed trees. It was a rude awakening from the dream of a settled pastorate. All experienced it, were dismayed at first, then took courage and soon rejoiced in the very crudity of a life offering opportunity to initiative and enterprise. They even commiserated their friends in the East for the quiet and humdrum character of *their* lives. Also they asserted that by environment they were "*compelled* to grow in mental strength, energy, breadth of views and high Christian aims." In answer to the argument of deprivation from the "privileges of refined society," they replied: "In your refined society, so-called, there is much that is artificial, formal, and sometimes hollow. *We* have learned that there is such a thing as being civilized and refined almost to death." The writer of these words, perhaps the most gentle and courteous member of the band, unconsciously reflected the very essence of the ideal qualities of democracy in the westward movement. Religion was renewing ·its vigor in this new nation of the West.

One can easily picture the joys of these young men in the opportunities of this young state. They were to mould Iowa in Christianity and they labored even to the limits of strength. The wife of one member, fragile, never suited physically to the hardships of frontier life, when urged to limit her exertions, answered, "Somebody must be built into these foundations,"—and this saying became almost a text for those who survived her. The great object was to establish churches, and one historian has written "no equal number of young ministers, leaving a theological seminary together, ever founded so many churches in five or ten years after their graduation as these men." But they felt equally the call of education, and even before leaving Andover one had said, "If each one of us can only plant one good permanent church, and all together build a college, what a work that would be." Less than six months after the Band reached Iowa, a ministers' meeting was called to discuss the founding of a college, and already imbued with Western enterprise, it was proposed to locate public lands, "boom" a college town, and thus provide the institution with funds. Eastern support was urged and denied for this real-estate enterprise, so the more cautious policy was followed of soliciting funds sufficient actually to start a college. By 1846, three years after reaching Iowa, a small fund having been raised, a college organization was perfected, one of the would-be land boomers putting a dollar on the table, saying, "Now appoint your trustees to take care of that dollar for Iowa College." In 1848 the college was established at Davenport, with one building costing $2000. In 1859 it was removed to a more central location at Grinnell, and, participating in the industrial development of the state, has become one of its strongest educational institutions.

It is impossible to do more than indicate in outline the influence of this home missionary movement in Iowa, stirred into vigor by the Band, and exercising a moral influence on every aspect of religious, social and political life. To all later workers in Iowa home missions, the Band set the standard of fearlessness in applying their religion to political issues. When they arrived in 1843, the agitation for statehood was just coming to the front, and soon the question of slavery was up for discussion in the territorial legislature. In the three years before statehood came, these young ministers boldly preached their faith in anti-slavery,—one of them had been, indeed, a member of that boys' abolition society which resulted in expulsion from Phillips Andover Academy. In the lecture on anti-slavery, I referred to a statement made by a speaker at the recent Historical Association meeting in Boston to the effect that in the years preceding the Civil War, pulpit utterances and church sentiment were opposed to the anti-slavery agitation. As to pulpit utterances available for study in the sermons of noted preachers, I have no comprehensive knowledge, but it would be an error in historical investigation to take the sermons of noted preachers as proof of the attitude of the *bulk* of the clergy,— the preachers in the small country church. One might get the impression from the card catalogue of Yale library that all the ministers of New England always printed all of their sermons. But this was not so in the West, and for Congregationalism in Iowa,—the dominating and all-powerful home missionary religious influence in that state,—I know that the whole *tradition* of the state asserts the moulding force of the country pastors in the anti-slavery agitation. For *written* proof of this tradition the historical investigator has but to turn to the minutes and resolutions of the annual association of the Congregational churches. There he will find, each year, resolutions adopted urging the ministers to attack intemperance, slavery, the Mexican War, national disruption threats, and like subjects. Religion, in this westward movement, did dare to apply to civic questions its ideals of moral conduct. Of one member of the Iowa Band, whose glory it was that in his old age he was known as "Father" to the people of Iowa, it was said, "no man, living or dead, has done more for Iowa than this good man."

The story of the Iowa Band is exceptional, because of its romantic inception, and vigorous labors in stirring times. It is, however, but one illustration of the great wave of home missionary energy expended in the new Western states, and I have told the story badly if it has not been made clear that here was a new attitude and a new emphasis in religious expression. Possibly, rather, I should term it a renewed attitude and emphasis. The home missionaries did not alter their creeds,— indeed, they often went out purposely to combat religious vagaries in creed. But they broke through the barrier that had separated the pulpit from the pew, prayed with their people, shared in their emotions and their ideals. This was the new attitude. The new emphasis lay in the placing of service above pulpit instruction. It came unsought, perhaps even unwelcomed, and was still largely unrecognized as the highest ideal of religion. But the germ of it sprouted in home missions.

This great religious movement was continued with energy up to the Civil War, and religion furnished moral ideals preparatory for the part the West was to play in that war. During its progress the pulpit everywhere again produced great spiritual leaders, inspired by national and moral ideals. War, it is claimed, always brings to the anxious watchers in the home a revival of religious emotion. Whatever the merits of this generalization, it is certain that during the Civil War, in both North and South, such a revival did occur, and that the pulpit renewed its vigor in spiritual leadership. I have not time even to enumerate the famous preachers of this day, and in illustration name but two, both of whom struck their highest note in expressing the ideal of nationality. Henry Ward Beecher, an eloquent and stirring pulpit orator, a moral guide to his people, was sent to England in 1863 to proclaim the ideals of anti-slavery and nationality for which the North was struggling. Thomas Starr King, whose name is still foremost in California as her "preacher patriot," by his enthusiasm and oratory in the crisis of 1861, impressed upon the state the indelible stamp of his spiritual leadership. He felt with all his soul the cause for the Union. Not a vigorous man, physically, he persisted in his labors in spite of the entreaties of friends, avowing that he had "enlisted for the war," and he did not survive to see its conclusion. These men, and many others, illustrate an unusual pulpit leadership in an unusual emergency. They used religion as a force in support of the ideal of nationality.

Like illustrations of the intensity of religious feeling and patriotism might be given for the South, though not from the lips of equally renowned preachers. The South also believed in the moral justice of its cause. But when the war had ended there came over the spirit of the reunited nation a sense of lethargy in ideals, whatever their nature. Nationality was reëstablished, but for other causes there was little enthusiasm. This was partly due to the exhaustion of emotion in the war, partly to the pressing necessity for industrial recuperation. For a time anti-slavery sentiment, fearing a virtual renewal of Southern slavery by labor laws, was kept alive in the reconstruction troubles. But by 1875, when it was seen that the South had no intention of reënslaving the negro, this ideal had waned also. The centennial celebration of 1876 was the occasion of much patriotic writing, expressing devout thankfulness for the mercies of Providence to America, and voicing faith in divine guidance. In his Centennial Hymn, Whittier wrote:

" Our fathers' God! from out whose hand
　The centuries fall like grains of sand,
　We meet to-day, united, free,
　And loyal to our land and Thee,
　To thank Thee for the era done,
　And trust Thee for the opening one.

　　　*　　*　　*　　*　　*

" Oh make Thou us, through centuries long,
　In peace secure, in justice strong;
　Around our gift of freedom draw
　The safeguards of Thy righteous law;
　And, cast in some diviner mould,
　Let the new cycle shame the old."

But such faith and hope lacked living stimulus.
The nation was apparently without ideals, save
those of industrial progress. Religion shared in
this apathy, spending its energy in seizing what it
could of the tide of national prosperity, erecting
splendid church edifices, and, as the close personal
contact of the pioneer days was lost in the growth
of towns and cities, retreating to the stronghold
of religious dogma. But creeds no longer satisfied
the ideals of the spirit. There was no living interest
in them,—no demand for a change of articles of
faith. This was so much true that today we find
it difficult to understand the heart-searchings, and
the doctrinal disputes that enlivened colonial times,
and even the earlier nineteenth century. Creeds,
it is often said, are the product of both religious
thought and religious feeling, and the time had

now come in America when the appeal of religion as a system of thought had lost its force.

The pulpit was the first to recover from this stagnant period in American idealism. Searching its own heart, and eager for a restored influence, it turned to that second element of religious life, never wholly lacking, but long overshadowed by doctrinal dispute,—the religious feeling of mankind,—the inherent necessity in every man's soul of expressing his sense of a relationship to a divine being, and a divine purpose. Up to this point I have sought to trace the force of religion in America in terms limited to Protestant faith and Protestant expression, and this is historically correct, for that faith alone had an intimate relationship to the other American ideals of the times. Other faiths had meanwhile gained adherents, notably Catholicism, but had been compelled to struggle for a right to exist, against the Protestant traditions, and had spent their energies in that contest. But Protestant prejudice, roused to extreme intolerance in the so-called "Know Nothing" political movement of the fifties, seeking to damn as "un-American" all other faiths, had fought and lost its battle. Freedom of conscience, in whatever faith, had triumphed, and all faiths now shared in the new endeavor to reanimate religion, placing a minor emphasis on an accepted system of religious thought, and appealing directly to the sense, or feeling of religion. Thus seeking for a restored influence, the pulpit, of whatever denomination or creed, offered *service by man to man*. This was not a new offering; it had always been present in religious teaching, but it was now given a place never before known in American history.

Let us review, briefly, the force of religion in our national ideals in the nineteenth century. It has been noted that democratic political institutions followed after, and were partly derived from democratic church organization. Then came the parallel development in church and state, of the ideals of personal liberty, each operating independently, yet each influencing the other. Next, followed the religious participation in nationality, both inspired by it, and contributing to it,—and later sharing as well in the ideals of anti-slavery and manifest destiny. In all of these ideals, religious conviction was present, and in some it led.

The purpose, and the limits of this lecture, devoted to the force of the ideal of religion, have not permitted me to dilate upon the changing aspects of the American theory of religion, but throughout, and in the summary just made, I have at least hinted at what I conceive these changes to have been, and to what conclusions they have now been brought. In my view, the religious instinct of mankind, during the nineteenth century in America, has been struggling to escape from the thrall of dogmatic theology, while an American ideal of religion was fortunately preserved by the participation of religion in the advance of democracy and nationality. But it is only today that we see clearly what has been the meaning of this century-long struggle,—what is, in truth, the essence of American religion. I find it best stated in the words of an English Roman Catholic, William Barry, though in some minor phrases, one can not agree. He writes:

"Americans once believed with shuddering in man's total depravity, from which only the small number of the elect were redeemed. They now believe that man is by nature good, by destiny perfect, and quite capable of saving himself. But in a sort of 'ideal America' they recognize the motive power of this more humane life toward which they ought ceaselessly to be tending. The Commonwealth is their goal, business their way to heaven, progress their duty, free competition their method. Mystery, obedience, self-denial are repugnant to them. But they admire self-discipline when it rejects what is beneath man's dignity, or, in deference to a fine idea, practices temperance. They are a breed of heroes rather than ascetics;" . . . To the American "The Divine Power is his Friend, not his Fate; and his belief in human nature as something of intrinsic value, to be made perfect hereafter, is the free acceptance of a Divine Idea which it is man's duty to realize. Thus civilization and Religion are but different facets of the same glory."

The full significance of this, the author's conclusion of his remarkable essay on "The Religion of America," can not be fully grasped in a single reading. In this lecture I have attempted to indicate historically the persistence throughout of the two basic truths in American religion,—faith in a Divine Idea, and a sense of duty to realize that idea,—expressing itself today in terms of humanity and service.

In the field of civic life and responsibility the ideal of religion was the first among American ideals to renew its vigor after the Civil War. It blazed the path guiding the nation to that sense of humanity which is today its highest ideal. There are those who still assert the decadence of religion as a force in American life. If I read history aright, it has always been a force, and in the last forty years has led men to a new and higher moral and civic consciousness. Whence came the wonderful modern development of societies and movements seeking to better the physical condition and enlarge the spiritual horizon of one's fellow men? From what initial energy sprang the settlement centers, self-help clubs, charitable societies, mission chapels, night schools, Christian associations, and all the rest of that long list of organizations rejoicing in service? *From pulpit leadership and from religious feeling.* One great recognized ideal of America today is service, and it is an active force, everywhere that thoughtful and spiritual-minded men work, in the professions, in business, in labor, in politics. Whatever the alleged vagaries or reactions of political parties, however distrustful one political leader may be of the sincerity of another, the fact remains that all parties and all leaders today claim an ideal quality for their policies, all assert that they would serve their fellow men, and all are truly animated by higher moral and political standards. The pulpit initiated the modern expression of this ideal; it met instant and ever increasing response in the nation's religious instincts; today service is the keynote of American religion.

> " O land of hope! thy future years
>   Are shrouded from our mortal sight;
> But thou canst turn the century's fears
>   To heralds of a cloudless light!
>
> *   *   *   *   *
>
> " O Spirit of immortal truth,
>   Thy power alone that circles all
> Can feed the fire as in its youth—
>   Can hold the runners lest they fall!"*

If churches, with spire, a church bell, and a permanent pastor, alone indicate the proportion of the people influenced by religious motive, it may be that religion has not kept pace with national

* "After the Centennial," by Christopher Pearce Cranch.

growth. I have made no comparison of statistics. But the instinct and the practice of service is first and always based on a sense of religion,—on a faith in divine purpose and in immortality. Without this faith,—driven to pessimism by the meagre results of the labors of one short life,—they would be few indeed who would follow the banner of service. But it is not the few today in America who follow that banner. The leaders are many, and the army is a multitude. Religion is still a National ideal. And in conclusion I venture a quotation, possibly become a commonplace to you here at Yale, but read with inspiration by one to whom it was unfamiliar, as embodying for us who constitute the rank and file of this army, the ideal of religion in service. On the tomb of Elihu Yale, in Wrexham Church Yard, North Wales, are these lines:

" Born in America, in Europe bred,
  In Africa travell'd, and in Asia wed,
  Where long he liv'd and thriv'd; in London dead.
  Much good, some ill, he did; so hope all's even,
  And that his soul thro' mercys gone to Heavn.
  You that survive and read this tale, take care,
  For this most certain exit to prepare:
  Where blest in peace, the actions of the just
  Smell sweet, and blossom in the silent dust."

V

DEMOCRACY—A VISION

V

DEMOCRACY—A VISION

Whereas in discussing other ideals, it has seemed necessary to prove their existence and force, in the present case both may be taken for granted. Democracy, as a powerful ideal, is acknowledged by all to have been a steady force in our history for over a hundred years, and is still a term of national inspiration. Mr. Justice Hughes, in his lectures on the Dodge Foundation in 1909, said:

"His study of history and of the institutions of his country has been to little purpose if the college man has not caught the vision of Democracy and has not been joined by the troth of heart and conscience to the great human brotherhood which is working out its destiny in this land of opportunity."

The *power* of this ideal, I therefore take for granted. I ask your attention rather to the *meaning* of Democracy as an American vision, seeking to note the changing aspects of that vision, and the conditions of such change.

The sources of the theory of democracy,—its origins, are to be found in religious faiths, and in America church organization paved the way for

the application of the theory to government. But
as a cult, the theory undoubtedly first found ade-
quate expression amongst us in the writings of
Thomas Paine. The appeal made by his works
was due to a remarkable combination of clear statement, vigorous and attractive writing, and a deduc-
tion from which there was no escape—provided one
granted his premises. Just arrived from England,
he published in 1776 his pamphlet "Common
Sense." It attracted instant attention, and 120,000
copies were sold in less than three months. His
biographer, Cheetham, seeking constantly to belittle
Paine's influence, yet says of "Common Sense":

"Speaking a language which the colonists had
felt but not thought, its popularity, terrible in its
consequences to the parent country, was unex-
ampled in the history of the press."

Long afterwards, Edmund Randolph analyzed
Paine's influence as due to "an imagination which
happily combined political topics," to a style new on
this side the Atlantic, and to sentiments already
germinating in American hearts. In 1790, having
returned to England, Paine wrote "The Rights of
Man" in answer to Burke on the French revolution.
Again he displayed a wonderful capacity to unite
ideals and close logic. In these two books Paine
was then the first to state the ideal of democracy,
as it later came to be accepted in America under

the leadership of Jefferson, though the political beliefs of the latter were independently developed and can not be ascribed directly to the influence of Paine's writings.

The patriotic orator fondly ascribes to the Declaration of Independence the ideals of democracy, finding them in the phrases:

"We hold these truths to be self-evident, that all men are created equal; that they are endowed by their Creator with certain unalienable rights; that among these are life, liberty, and the pursuit of happiness."

The men who signed that declaration, however, were far from intending a profession of faith either in the absolute equality of mankind, or even in the equality of political rights. If they had sought at all to elucidate their meaning, they would have stated it in terms of equality before the law. Not even Jefferson was prepared for human equality. The declaration was rather, as it has been aptly characterized, a campaign document, setting forth certain attractive generalities intended to arouse popular support, and enumerating specific grievances against King George III. The vital democratic sentiment of America was not aroused, in fact, until at least twenty years after the Declaration of Independence, and the one principle of that earlier platform, then elevated to the dignity of a

creed, was that of "liberty," with Jefferson as its
high priest.

Ever since 1800 the name of Thomas Jefferson
has been associated with democracy, both as an
ideal in itself, and as an ideal form of government.
What then was *his vision* of democracy? It was
simply a faith in personal liberty as the highest
guiding principle in the progress of civilization.
This was the center and sum of his entire philosophy. His purpose was, always and ever, to
guard the liberty of the individual. He had no vital
conception of the force of those other catch-words
of the French revolution,—"equality," and "fraternity." Contrary to the accusations of his political
opponents, he was not a disciple of French philosophy, though his residence in France, and his
habit of mind, gave him a clear view of the inner
meaning of the French revolution, and made him
tolerant of its crudities. This, then, being *his*
vision of democracy, he found in popular sovereignty and the rule of the majority, the governmental principles most likely to secure the ideal
of personal liberty.

This vision, and this medium of realization, are
constantly reiterated in all that Jefferson wrote, or
said, or did. Yet Jefferson's writings, frequently
spoken of as if they constituted volumes of a care-
fully organized philosophy, are, in fact, save for
one book and a few state papers, merely a collection

of his thirty thousand private letters. The book is his "Notes on Virginia," while the Declaration of Independence, two inaugural addresses, and several state papers make up the sum of his formal writing. Nevertheless it is not inaccurate to speak of the influence of Jefferson's writings, for in truth they have been a greater force in American political thinking than all the publications of all the other presidents combined, simply because he set up the one single ideal of liberty in government and in religion, and never wavering from it in theory (though at times inconsistent in practice), constantly drove it home in intimate talk and correspondence. Jefferson prided himself on the fearlessness of his thought, stating that he "never feared to follow truth and reason, to whatever results they led, and bearding every authority which stood in their way," but he rarely put that thought into formal writing. At his first inauguration, however, March 4, 1801, he stated his principles. Pleading for good temper and conciliation in political controversies, which he contended were but ephemeral matters, he turned to liberty as the one desirable object of all government. This, he said, is to be secured by "absolute acquiescence in the decisions of the majority, the vital principle of republics, from which there is no appeal but to force, the vital principle and immediate parent of despotism."

I suppose that today nine tenths of those who talk of Jeffersonian democracy, postulate the Jeffersonian theory in terms of their own conceptions. Men once talked of "natural rights,"—and ascribed to nature their own mental visions. Just so, today, men attribute to Jefferson their own ideals of democracy. But to Jefferson, let it be repeated, the object of government was to secure the liberty of the individual, the only side of the prism which he saw clearly,—and democratic government was to him but the best method of realizing that ideal. Such government was not to him a perfect thing in itself, was not an Utopia. I have just quoted his words on the rule of majorities, but these did not imply Jefferson's belief that the decision of the majority was necessarily right. To believe that, is to believe in democracy as Utopia. In this same inaugural address he said:

"All too will bear in mind this sacred principle, that though the will of the majority is in all cases to prevail, that will, to be rightful must be reasonable; that the minority possess their equal rights which equal laws must protect, and to violate which would be oppression."

John Fiske has compressed Jefferson's theory of government into the statement that he had "strong faith in the teachableness of the great mass of the people." Such faith implies a belief in the wisdom of universal suffrage, but this is not at all to believe that "the voice of the people is the voice of God." And Jefferson himself indicated democratic government as merely a form preferable to other forms, when he stated:

"Sometimes it is said, that man cannot be trusted with the government of himself. Can he then be trusted with the government of others? Or, have we found angels in the form of kings to govern him? Let history answer this question."

Jefferson's vision of democracy was of one ideal—liberty, and of a form of government which, judged by *history,* not by any theory of natural right, was best suited to that ideal. If I have been unduly repetitious in stating this, let the excuse be the later error, that Jefferson proposed to find an Utopia in democracy.

Opposed to the theory that democracy was the handservant of liberty, there existed, in 1800, a sincere belief with some, that aristocratic government, or the government of the wise, was to be preferred, in the cause of this same liberty. The political success of Jefferson seemed to mark a backward rather than a forward step. Fisher Ames said in 1803:

"Our country is too big for Unión, too sordid for patriotism, too democratic for liberty. . . . Its vice will govern it by practising upon its folly. This is ordained for democracies."

But in spite of prophecies of evil the nation found inspiration in Jefferson's theories, and from his time on, has held them as a faith. New attributes were added in the popular mind, and that of equality, at least of equality of opportunity, soon came to exercise a more powerful influence in support of the ideal, than that of liberty. America had, indeed, a very confused notion of what it meant in acclaiming democracy. Nationality, special destiny, religious and political liberty, equality of opportunity, industrial prosperity, were all jumbled in the idealization of that democracy which America alone was held to possess. To most foreign visitors about 1830, America seemed to have gone mad in a craze for democracy, as necessarily the wisest and best type of government. Captain Hall summed up his argument against this faith by citing a part of the thirty-eighth chapter of the Book of Ecclesiasticus, in the Apocrypha, beginning,

"The wisdom of a learned man cometh by opportunity of leisure; and he that hath little business shall become wise."

"How can he get wisdom that holdeth the plough, and that glorieth in the goad? That driveth oxen, and is occupied in their labours, and whose talk is of bullocks?"

This thought is always a common one to conservative and cultivated men, who exalt good administration as the end of all government. The answer for democracy is that even though there be a poorer administration and a seeming slower progress (though this is usually denied), the freedom of a democratic government from violent upheavals,—its safety-valve qualities,—make it in the long run the superior medium of development. But the American people of 1830 did not content themselves with any such defense of democracy. Jacksonian democracy clamorously proclaimed its faith, and sincerely believed that in the election of its hero, the nation has been torn from the control of an aristocratic and moneyed class.   Webster wrote of Jackson's inauguration: "I never saw such a crowd before. . . . They really seem to think that the country is rescued from some dreadful danger." Sumner, the unsympathetic biographer of Jackson, says of the election of 1828, that it seemed truly to many Democrats, a rising of the people "in their might to overthrow an extravagant, corrupt, aristocratic, federalist administration, which had encroached on the liberties of the people," yet history adjudges the preceding administration of John Quincy Adams, as one of the purest, politically, ever known to us.

I attempt no examination of the many rivulets of interests and emotions that merged in the great stream of this new democratic vision. All that I can do here is to name a few of the larger tributaries. The bulk of Jackson's support came from the West, where *equality* had long existed, and from the Eastern cities, where it was desired. The new Democratic party, casting off the supremacy of intellectual leadership in the old, was a "poor man's party"—as Schouler has described it. The belief was widespread that an aristocracy had ruled this nation and that its support of democracy was but a false profession to delude the people. The West asserted that equality of opportunity in occupying public lands was denied it by the East. There was everywhere a spirit of revolt from tradition and authority. These were a few of the main sources of the new democracy. But running through each and all of these was a new vision of democracy,— an assertion that the people had never yet ruled themselves, that they were now to do so, that this rule of the average man necessarily must result not merely in better, but in a perfect government. The ideals of Jeffersonian democracy were primarily political. Those of Jacksonian democracy were both political and social, and in the newer, America, professing allegiance to equality, came closer to the French conception of democracy,— stated in terms of "liberty, equality, and fraternity," though to the majority of men, fraternity held but a vague meaning, since it seemed uncalled for in this "land of opportunity." Jeffersonian democracy held no thesis of social perfection. The new democracy, though sprouting from the older, was less an emergence than a new birth, for it elevated the form of government to an ideal that would assure both political and social Utopia.

After 1840, except for a few protesting voices, this new conception of the destiny of democracy was well-nigh universal in American life. America swelled with pride in the belief that she alone had solved the problem of human happiness under government, and that she led the world in ideals. As immigrants from foreign lands, driven by hunger in Ireland or by political oppression in Germany, poured into the country, America expanded the vision of her democracy into a haven of refuge, where all the races of the world might share in her peace and prosperity. Bryant's poem, "Oh Mother of a Mighty Race," expressed this vision:

> " There's freedom at thy gates and rest
> For earth's down-trodden and opprest,
> A shelter for the hunted head,
> For the starved laborer toil and bread.
>   Power, at thy bounds,
> Stops and calls back his baffled hounds."

Whenever a people rejoice in the conviction that they are a *favored* people, occupying the summit of

civilization, they are inspired by their very superiority to show their preëminence in every possible
way. The period of the forties, says Commons in his
History of American Industrial Society, was that
in which American fads and reforms ran riot. In
every city there were weekly meetings of societies
advocating anti-slavery, temperance, graham bread,
prison reform, woman's suffrage, dress reform,
"diffusion of bloomers," spiritualism, land reform,—while Brook Farm, Mormonism, Owenism
attracted less numerous, but equally enthusiastic
followers. "It was," he asserts, "the golden age
of the talk-fest, the lycéum, the brotherhood of
man,—the 'hot air' period of American history."
But we should also note that it was the period of
an outburst of intellectual and spiritual ideals of
permanent force and value. American literature,
for example, flowered in the forties, in the new
sense of American nationality and idealism. Sporadic and temporary reform movements always
appear in the whirlpool of a new national enthusiasm. Gradually the froth disappears, while the
deep current moves on. For a time manifest destiny was at the surface, then anti-slavery replaced
it, while far down, more dense in volume, lay the
sense of nationality and religion, permeated with
an ideal vision of democracy.

In the first lecture of this series, I stated that it
was the ideal of nationality, which stood suddenly

revealed in all its power, by the attack on Fort Sumter, uniting the North. But in the Civil War, though less clearly recognized, there was also a conflict between two ideals of democracy. We in America understood this but dimly, while to the interested English observer it seemed very clear. The South held the theory of a democracy of wise men, that is, in practice, of an intellectual aris- tocracy,—directly opposed to the Northern ideal of a government of average men. Also America had so boasted its superiority in government that the mere disruption of the Union seemed to deny the efficacy of democratic institutions. The crisis in America was thus of intense interest to English- men in its relation to their own problems of political organization, for just as the war began, the pressure of a reform party, largely basing its arguments on the success of democracy in America, was beginning to threaten the supremacy of an aristocratic govern- ment, not altered since the Reform Bill of 1832. Thus Englishmen had a domestic political interest in our struggle, defended their views according to that interest, and clearly expressed their sense that "democracy was on trial." At first confident that the North could never conquer the South, aristo- cratic sentiment was later made anxious by the campaigns on the Mississippi, and when the news came that Sherman had reached the sea at Savan- nah, the editor of the *London Times,* Delane, foreseeing the victory of the North, and dreading the influence on English politics, wrote to the prime minister, Palmerston, "The American news is a heavy blow to us as well as to the South." Lord Acton, clinging to the vision of a government of the wise, wrote, "I broke my heart over the surrender of Lee." On the other hand, John Bright, radical advocate of a British expansion of the franchise, deserted his seat in parliament to tour the country, seeking to arouse sympathy with the North, and picturing the struggle in America as one which involved the future of the democratic principle. He appealed especially to the starving cotton operatives of Lancashire, and they gave evidence of their faith by refraining from a turbulence that might have encouraged the English government to interfere on the side of the South. Karl Marx labored among the workmen of London for like reasons. The personality of Lincoln soon assumed to Englishmen the significance of a political demonstration. If a man sprung from the crudest surroundings, with no education, no heritage of administrative powers, uncouth in appearance, hitherto unskilled in the conduct of affairs of state, could guide a nation safely through the stress of a civil war, then indeed democracy would have proved its value. So at least argued English observers. To the English governing classes, Lincoln,—the real Lincoln,—was a myth. English credulity could not go so far as to accept, or comprehend, such a man. Punch, in numerous cartoons, exhibited him, first as the incompetent fool striving to be a man, later, when his strength became clear, as a despot crushing the liberties of America. But when our soldiers North and South, after Lee's surrender, hastened to resume their former occupations, prophecies of a military despotism were set at naught, the force of the ideal of democracy was fully recognized, and Lincoln came to be regarded as its highest, its marvelous demonstration. Four lines of Tom Taylor's beautiful poem in Punch,—his recantation for four years of injustice to Lincoln,—sum up the new British comprehension:

> " Yes, he had lived to shame me from my sneer,
>   To lame my pencil, and confute my pen—
>   To make me own this hind of princes peer,
>   This rail splitter a true born King of men."

England believed, then, what we did not clearly understand, that the war was a contest between two differing ideals of democracy, and involved the fate of the democratic form of government as well. As to the last, I think England unduly magnified the possible results of the conflict. Our very lack of any feeling that democratic government was at stake is evidence of its complete obsession amongst us. Both during and after the war we simply took democracy for granted, and rested secure in the faith that our *form* of government, a divinely ordained machine, would correct all evils.

All ideals shared in the intellectual and moral lethargy of the next period, and politics, in which ideals find their most far-reaching expression, fell, by the neglect of the duties of citizenship, into the hands of men not representative of a living democracy. The "boss," to the dismay of America, assumed a power and proportions hitherto unknown, but we were long in waking to his real significance in the theory of democracy. Still enthralled with the *vision* of democracy as Utopia, where, without effort in citizenship, the mere acceptance of a right theory of government must *work* right, America merely smiled at Lowell's epigram on "The Boss":

> " Skilled to pull wires, he baffles Nature's hope,
> Who sure intended him to stretch a rope."

America listened respectfully to Huxley's sharp criticism in his farewell speech at New York, but his caution, "eternal suspicion is the price of liberty," was soon forgotten in the flood tide of industrial prosperity.

The first note of doubt in this peaceful and passive confidence in an ideal was aroused by the inrush of a new immigration, more difficult of absorption than the old. Aldrich, in his poem

"Unguarded Gates," gave warning of perils hitherto unheeded.

> " O Liberty, white Goddess! is it well
> To leave the gates unguarded? On thy breast
> Fold Sorrow's children, soothe the hurts of fate,
> Lift the down-trodden, but with hands of steel
> Stay those who to thy sacred portals come
> To waste the gifts of freedom. Have a care
> Lest from thy brow the clustered stars be torn
> And trampled in the dust. For so of old
> The thronging Goth and Vandal trampled Rome,
> And where the temples of the Cæsars stood
> The lean wolf unmolested made her lair."

By 1890, American apathy had disappeared. Aroused by the problem of this new immigration,—with that great solvent, the public land, exhausted,—with new and unexpected transformations in the industrial world,—above all, with a new generation of citizens, seeking again, as had their fathers in their youth, ideals by which to guide their conduct, the nation awakened from the dream that democracy, without effort, cures all ills.

The first result of this rude awakening was reaction against the ideal itself. The vision had failed in part,—it must be altogether wrong. In its place was raised the ideal of "good administration," which, let it be established by whatever manipulation, even trickery, was justified of its works. Though proclaimed discreetly, this was but the old ideal of government by the wisest,—an ideal whose fatal defect is that it must, in the end, be maintained by despotic force. Nor was the reaction against democracy confined to America. Since the middle of the nineteenth century, Europe also had professed her faith in the vision, and yet had seen new times give birth to new evils. In England, especially, popular self-government, manhood suffrage, had been preached as a panacea for national diseases, and beginning with the Reform Bill of 1867, the solution of every difficulty had been sought in a farther expansion of the franchise. The ardent political reformers of the mid-century themselves believed, and imposed their faith upon the nation, that popular government assured perfection. Failing to realize a perfect society, these same leaders, their youthful dreams shattered, sounded the note of distrust in their own earlier ideals. Permit me to expand and restate this general reaction by paraphrase and citation from the Dodge Lectures of 1908 by Mr. Bryce. This distinguished publicist there traces the history of the ideal of democracy, stating that in the later eighteenth century, and the earlier nineteenth, there was in America a devoted faith in government of the people by the people. In spite of those who doubted, and whose doubts placed in our constitution checks upon hastily considered popular action, this faith became a creed. It produced in America a great sympathy with the

European revolutions of 1830 and 1848. In Europe itself there was passionate expression of belief in a democracy that would secure "a reign of brotherhood and peace, an age of tranquil prosperity and assured order." Since 1870, says Mr. Bryce, there has been reaction. Even though conditions of life and happiness have undoubtedly improved, there has been disappointment. The ills of society under other governmental forms have, indeed, disappeared, but new ills have replaced them. "The citizens have failed to respond to the demand for active virtue and intelligent public spirit which free government makes and must make. Everywhere there is the same contrast between that which the theory of democracy requires and that which the practice of democracy reveals." It is, he continues, the "average man" who is responsible. "The government is his. Officials are only his agents, working under his eye. The principles of a democracy ascribe and must ascribe to him the supreme and final voice in the conduct of public affairs. He can not disclaim his responsibility without the risk of forfeiting his rights."

These are wise words addressed to young men about to assume the duties of citizenship, but in one respect I think they are in error. They still proclaim the vision of an impossible democracy,—a vision of Utopia. "Everywhere," says Mr. Bryce, "there is the same contrast between that which the theory of democracy requires and that which the practice of democracy reveals." He, too, inspired in youth by a vision of governmental perfection, now experiences the reaction from failure to reach that goal. For many, such reaction results in outright pessimism. I well remember a conversation, some years ago, with one who, about 1850, had been an enthusiast in the cause of a wider franchise in England. "Do you in America," he said, "still believe in democracy?" and then added, "I once had faith in it also."

If this Utopian ideal of democracy is the thing to be tested, then, indeed "that which the theory of democracy requires" is sadly lacking in "that which the practice of democracy reveals." *But there was a fallacy in the vision.* It misled men, for there is no human perfection, and there is, and can be, no such thing on earth as perfect government. Society is an organism, changing, growing, putting off old forms, and putting on new ones. The true test of democracy is not fulfilment; it is progressive betterment. Let us return to the average man. Who that knows the history of Europe will deny that in intelligence, in humanity, in toleration, in sympathy, in physical comforts, in respect for the government under which he lives,—his own government, because he owns it,—the average man of the twentieth century is far superior to his brother of a hundred years ago? This is not to assert that these betterments are exclusively the products of democracy, but that under democracy they have grown with a rapidity unknown to any other form of governmental institutions.

In America, up to 1870 at least, there was the same advance, after which there was a resting time in the world of spirit, partly due indeed to our very exaggeration of the ideal of democracy,—to our fallacious belief in an impossible vision. Today we see more clearly both the merits and the limitation of democracy. Political liberty, equality before the law, fraternity in human sympathy, we may hope to secure through government. Industrial liberty, equality of opportunity, must yield in part, at least, to the organic sense of the nation,—to fraternity. Political parties in America are today divided, in theory, by the differing limits they would place on industrial liberty and equality of opportunity, but they are in agreement that some limit is necessary, and the cause of this agreement is a higher appreciation of the ideal of fraternity. This is our American conception of social democracy, but we no longer hold it perfect in itself,—it is but progress toward some unseen goal. Today, youth again asserting its faith in ideals, the nation reawakened, gropes to resume the path of betterment, and it has this advantage over an earlier time, that its view is clearer, its method more sane, since men,—even average men,—have cast aside the dream of democracy as the perfect state, but still cling to it, and exalt it in government, as the safest means of steady, peaceful advance.

It is beyond the scope of this lecture, and beyond my privilege, to indicate the lines of this new advance. There are many faiths, and as many priests, who would willingly serve as guides. On one basic principle all are united,—that democracy, long content to make liberty its one ideal, asserting the privilege and the rights of the individual in society, means today, rather, a conception of society where the ideal of fraternity rests side by side with that of liberty, where duty shares with rights. But my text has been simply the vision of democracy, and in tracing its advance in America, if I have denied it qualities ascribed to it in earlier times, it is because of faith in it as an ideal medium of development. My text is, then, "Faith in Democracy," not to be unfairly tested by the impossible standards of perfection, but judged as a progressively bettered organism, with a healthier body, a mind more open to reason, and a soul more sensitive to ideals.

In concluding this, the last lecture on *The Power of Ideals in American History,* permit me a word in recapitulation. Some of the ideals I have touched upon are not now influential in national life. It would be idle today to appeal to anti-slavery sentiment in the sense in which it was understood in the fifties. Manifest destiny, so far as the craze for territorial expansion is concerned, is fortunately no longer an obsession, though we wisely cling to belief in a high spiritual destiny. These ideals, as formerly expressed, were suited to particular occasions, and have passed away. But this in no way weakens the statement of their force while they existed, nor lessens the truth of the conclusion that ideals have powerfully affected the course of our history. Indeed, one may go beyond this and, though proving by analysis and historical study that an ideal was conceived in error, and wrong in application, may yet postulate the political, even the moral, force of the ideal itself. This fact I have just attempted to make clear in relation to some supposed attributes of the ideal of democracy. Briefly, my purpose throughout has not been to proclaim certain ideals as in themselves always admirable, but to assert their force, and by inference to prove that since America has never been without ideals, she cannot today dispense with them. If this be accepted, it follows that every one, especially every young man, should feel the duty of self-examination, seeking to discover his own ideals and sentiments toward national problems and personal life. Having so discovered them he must, if he be a real man, seek to translate them into action. Thus fulfilling his duty as a citizen he will help to mould his country, and to preserve it from wreck in times of crisis. For it is in such times that ideals and sentiments rule, and decide the fate of peoples and of states.

Three ideals treated in these lectures still live in America. Religion, a faith in divine purpose, finds satisfaction in this life, in service. It is the fountain head of all ideals, and we may state our belief with Lowell: "Moral supremacy is the only one that leaves monuments and not ruins behind it." Democracy, not as Utopia but as the best method of steady progress, and with new emphasis upon fraternity, permeates our national consciousness. Nationality is still the most powerful political sentiment in the United States, and in the whole world. Those who would discard it among the nations of the earth are visionary, for the time is so remote when the sentiment of nationality will have disappeared, as to be beyond the vision of the great mass of men. But nationality to us means more than union in government; it means union in all American ideals, the moral assets of the nation. With Longfellow we profess our faith:

> "Thou, too, sail on, O Ship of State!
> Sail on, O Union, strong and great!
> Humanity with all its fears,
> With all the hopes of future years,
> Is hanging breathless on thy fate!

> *   *   *   *   *   *

Fear not each sudden sound and shock,
'Tis of the wave and not the rock;
'Tis but the flapping of the sail,
And not a rent made by the gale!
In spite of rock and tempest's roar,
In spite of false lights on the shore,
Sail on, nor fear to breast the sea!
Our hearts, our hopes, are all with thee,
Our hearts, our hopes, our prayers, our tears,
Our faith triumphant o'er our fears,
Are all with thee,—are all with thee."

INDEX

INDEX